Sexual Politics in Contemporary Europe

Sharron FitzGerald · May-Len Skilbrei

Sexual Politics in Contemporary Europe

Moving Targets, Sitting Ducks

Sharron FitzGerald
Department of Criminology &
Sociology of Law,
University of Oslo
Oslo, Norway

May-Len Skilbrei
Department of Criminology &
Sociology of Law
University of Oslo
Oslo, Norway

ISBN 978-3-030-91173-7   ISBN 978-3-030-91174-4 (eBook)
https://doi.org/10.1007/978-3-030-91174-4

© The Author(s), under exclusive license to Springer Nature Switzerland AG 2022
This work is subject to copyright. All rights are solely and exclusively licensed by the Publisher, whether the whole or part of the material is concerned, specifically the rights of translation, reprinting, reuse of illustrations, recitation, broadcasting, reproduction on microfilms or in any other physical way, and transmission or information storage and retrieval, electronic adaptation, computer software, or by similar or dissimilar methodology now known or hereafter developed.
The use of general descriptive names, registered names, trademarks, service marks, etc. in this publication does not imply, even in the absence of a specific statement, that such names are exempt from the relevant protective laws and regulations and therefore free for general use.
The publisher, the authors and the editors are safe to assume that the advice and information in this book are believed to be true and accurate at the date of publication. Neither the publisher nor the authors or the editors give a warranty, expressed or implied, with respect to the material contained herein or for any errors or omissions that may have been made. The publisher remains neutral with regard to jurisdictional claims in published maps and institutional affiliations.

This Palgrave Macmillan imprint is published by the registered company Springer Nature Switzerland AG
The registered company address is: Gewerbestrasse 11, 6330 Cham, Switzerland

Acknowledgements

This book is the result of our individual and combined thinking on gender and sexuality over the last decade or so. As feminist scholars we have become increasingly invested in understanding the origins, working and consequences of sexual politics in our time. While having different disciplinary backgrounds, our mutual starting position is the promotion of feminist critique and we share a research background in studying policy processes on sex work, human trafficking, migration and rape.

We thank our team at Palgrave for their enthusiasm for the project and support. The book emerges as part of our involvement in the project 'Evidently Rape', which is funded as a strategic project by the University of Oslo. The project and our work has been hosted by the Department of Criminology and Sociology of Law at the University of Oslo, where FitzGerald is currently a visiting scholar and Skilbrei a Professor. At the University of Oslo, we have received support in preparing the manuscript from Kamilla Kristiansen and Maja Vestad. We would like to thank them.

Writing a book, even a short one like this, takes a lot of time, attention and energy. We are blessed with caring and generous partners who listen to our complaints, rub our feet and buy us chocolate and wine. Thank you, Rolf and Ove, with love.

Oslo
September 2021

Sharron FitzGerald
May-Len Skilbrei

Contents

1 **Introduction: Reframing the Permissive Moment**   1
    Drilling Down into European Norms and Values Around
    Gender and Sexuality   8
    References   15

2 **On the Road to Lisbon: Europe Becoming a Normative**
    Community   19
    Establishing an Ever Closer Union Among the People
    of Europe   20
    How Can We Understand European Policy Processes Around
    Gender and Sexuality?   27
    The Role of Civil Society Actors   31
    Conclusion: Where to Now for European Gender
    and Sexuality Policy?   35
    References   39

3 **From Sweden to Brussels: Forging a European Agenda**
    on Prostitution   45
    A Genealogy of European Governance of Prostitution   46
    The Evolution of the 'Nordic Model'   53
    Shifting Feminist Prostitution Politics at the EU Level   58
    Conclusion: Prostitution and Its Place in Wider Sexual
    Politics   65
    References   66

4	**What Kind of Problematic Is Rape for the EU?**	73
	Positioning Rape in the EU Political Imaginary	76
	Establishing 'A European' Position on VAW	81
	The EU's Hard and Soft Approach to VAW	87
	Conclusion: Rethinking EU Responses to Sexual Violence	93
	References	94
5	**Forging National Sexual Politics: A Dance of Moving Targets and Sitting Ducks**	101
	Learning from Thy Neighbours	104
	Resistance to EU Normative Alignment	111
	European and Domestic Responses to the Threat of 'the Outside' and the 'Outsider Within'	116
	Conclusion: Is an Ever Closer Union on Track in the EU?	120
	References	120
6	**Sexual Politics in Contemporary Europe: Resonance and Dissonance**	125
	References	131
Index		133

CHAPTER 1

Introduction: Reframing the Permissive Moment

Abstract The Introduction establishes the book's primary focus, namely the current political 'moment' in European sexual politics. The chapter provides an important vehicle for introducing the reader to a new theoretical framework and a critical feminist analysis of the various dimensions of the political nature of gender and sexuality in Europe. It does this by interrogating the gendered and sexual nature of politics and governance between the European Union (EU) and its Member States. It begins by mapping the EU's policy for harmonisation around gender and sexual norms and values that allows for an examination of the implications of changes in European sexual politics for both social debates around gender and sexuality in general in contemporary Europe, and for feminist critique in particular relative to the complex discursive and material practices around gender and sexuality, including debates around identity, cultural politics and citizenship. The Introduction sets out the structure of the book.

Keywords Sexual politics · The EU · Harmonisation · Norms · Values · Feminism · Foucault-sexuality-bodies-biopower-governmentality

© The Author(s), under exclusive license to Springer Nature Switzerland AG 2022
S. FitzGerald and M.-L. Skilbrei, *Sexual Politics in Contemporary Europe*, https://doi.org/10.1007/978-3-030-91174-4_1

> There is no necessary connection between political decision making and moral change: politics is not a simple reflection of changes in society. But the political context in which decisions are made—to legislate or not, to prosecute or ignore—can be important in promoting shifts in the sexual regime and these have to be analysed both in terms of long-term shifts and in conjunctural terms. The law of unintended consequences can be as decisive as careful legislative intervention. (Weeks, 2012: 19)

Jeffrey Weeks in his seminal book, *Sex, Politics and Society*, explores how the 1960s and the beginning of the 1970s appear as a 'permissive moment' in Western Europe (2012: 321). His assessment resonates with shifts in wider societal attitudes around gender and sexuality[1] throughout Western Europe at the time. He suggested that in the post-world war two era, young people rejected what they perceived as previous generations' moral conservatism and, as a consequence, they rose up and challenged what they identified as their illiberal norms and behaviours. Weeks (2012) understood this framing as paradigmatic of western societies' assumptions about the sexual revolution as being liberating for all. He suggested, however, that this discursive shift did not happen overnight, but rather it was due to a 'long, still unfinished, revolution in erotic and intimate life that saw radical change in laws, attitudes and personal behaviour' (Weeks, 2012: 321). Weeks (2012) argued that these shifts in gender and sexual mores contributed to but were not the principle driving force that made this social transformation possible. Put simply, they were entwined with, but were not driving, wider societal developments, including demographic shifts. Some feminists have argued that the permissive moment did not crystallise into liberation for all, but rather it was sexual liberation on white men's terms, and that it 'contributed less to women's freedom' and more to their continued oppression' (Vance, 1992: 302). Western societies continue to interpret these changes as victories for all, including the women's and the gay liberation movements.

Sexual Politics in Contemporary Europe explores the various dimensions of those wider 'developments'. Before proceeding we want to stress that we do not claim to offer the definitive answer to the progress of European sexual politics. But rather we view this book as a spring board to develop a unique feminist theoretical framework that can open the

---

[1] Following Dunphy (2000), we understand 'sexuality' as the performance of sexual acts (having sex) *and* sexual identities. We apply both meanings.

door to a wider discussion on what is a pressing issue across Europe today. With these parameters in mind and throughout the book, we will apply the concept of 'sexual politics' as a discursive framework to define and encompass the political nature of gender and sexuality and the gendered and sexual nature of politics in Europe. We use this discursive framework to question the implications of changes in European sexual politics for both social and political debates around gender and sexuality in general in contemporary Europe, and for feminist critique in particular relative to the complex discursive and material practices around gender and sexuality, including debates around identity, cultural politics and citizenship. To assess the situation, we will drill down into *why* and *how* the European Union (EU) uses notions of 'appropriate' gender and sexual norms and values to push particular policy agendas and how, in turn, EU Member States and other actors, including feminists, adopt or resist these policy agendas. This is a subject about which scholars have written extensively (Bell & Binne, 2000; Knill & Preidel, 2015; Mepschen & Duyvendak, 2012; Stychin, 2003), and it is not our intention in this book to explore in any great detail the technicalities of policymaking at the EU and national levels. Instead, our approach is predicated upon a critical feminist analysis that uses, as an entry point for analysis, the argument that the permissive moment in European sexual politics is not the result of societies becoming 'less' moralistic and 'more' tolerant, but rather that it is a consequence of *why* and *how* these societies are re-organising their understanding of gender and sexuality relative to wider cultural and national identity politics and agendas. As Herzog observes, during the twentieth-century, sexuality has become 'burdened with enormous significance' (2011: 2; see also Foucault, 1980). The importance of this interpretation for our objectives is that it draws attention to how EU law and policy-makers implicate gender and sexuality norms and values to institutionalise a European political identity. It is this more nuanced reading of European sexual politics that allows for a recognition of the manner, in which EU policy-makers invoke discourses of gender and sexuality in the pursuit of greater harmonisation around law and policy across the Union.

In this book, we focus on how governance occurs in the interactions between different levels of European governance. We submit that how nation states collaborate or disagree over issues of gender and sexuality is meaningful because these are issues of both supranational, national and personal importance. What draws us to study European sexual politics is that 40 years after the so-called sexual revolution, we observe that irrespective of the EU's desire for policy harmonisation established in the Treaty of Amsterdam (EC 1997)[2] on issues around the economy, criminal justice and social policies, different Member States understand and attempt to regulate sexuality and gender relations differently. This situation continues to evolve. This means that in contemporary European societies, issues that governments and the law interpreted have previously understood as 'private' have become 'public' concerns and responsibilities. Similarly, lives that governments and laws have treated as 'deviant' and even criminal, have become, in certain European countries, normalised (Mattson, 2015). As researchers demonstrate, national developments relative to tolerance and protection around gender and sexuality are not straightforward (Euchner, 2019; Lister et al., 2007; Plummer, 2003). Simultaneously, as gender and sexuality are becoming prominent policy areas on the EU's agenda (Locher & Prügl, 2009), we observe a backlash from some Member States over gender equality policies and rights for Lesbian, Gay, Bisexual, Transgender, Queer and Intersex (LGBTQI) people across Europe. For example, the political right is building its regional and domestic powerbase around its rejection of these norms (Paternotte & Kuhar, 2017).

In the current 'political moment' of European sexual politics, then we observe the rise of politicised religion and a subsequent neo-traditionalism in several European countries, particularly those located in the former Soviet Bloc (Le Roux, 2017). Recent controversies between the EU and Member States such as Poland bring the schism into sharp relief. For example in June 2020, the Polish government announced its withdrawal from the Council of Europe Convention on Preventing and Combating Violence against Women and Domestic Violence (2011) (often referred to as the Istanbul Convention).[3] The Convention formulates demands on signatory countries to apply particular definitions of and punishments for manifestations of gendered power. In response, the Polish government argues that it has withdrawn from the Convention because it 'does not respect religion and promotes controversial ideologies about gender'. Addressing questions around Poland's decision to withdraw, the Polish

---

[2] Available at: https://eur-lex.europa.eu/legal-content/EN/TXT/?uri=CELEX:11997D/TXT. Accessed 4 September 2020.

[3] Available at: https://www.coe.int/en/web/conventions/full-list/-/conventions/rms/090000168008482e?module=treaty-detail&treatynum=210. Accessed 4 September 2020.

Justice Minister, Zbigniew Ziobro, describes the Convention as 'harmful' because it requires that schools teach children about gender from 'a sociological point of view'.[4] Although the Minister did not elaborate on what this view entailed, his message was clear: EU norms and values around gender and sexuality were incongruous with a particular Polish national identity.

This situation illustrates how discourses on gender and sexuality animate, but also have the potential to derail, the European project. Paternotte and Kuhar note that the backlash against how the EU is forging 'a European position' on gender and sexuality has surprised many in Brussels and in EU institutions (2017: 3). They suggest that the EU assume that Europe 'was on an unstoppable way towards "full" gender equality and sexual citizenship' (Paternotte & Kuhar, 2017: 3). They suggested that the EU assumed that 'opposition was largely foreign to the European experience or could only subsist as a reminder of the past, primarily in Eastern Europe or in (Catholic) countries such as Italy or Ireland' (Paternotte & Kuhar, 2017: 3). This suggests that, while European resistance to gender equality and LGBTQI rights are particularly visible in these kinds of actions, including legal actions in Hungary and Poland, such sentiments and demonstrations operate also beyond these 'usual suspects'.

Alongside a discussion of the role that gender and sexuality play in the construction and constitution of a contemporary European political identity, it is equally important to consider the power structures, relationships and processes that have emerged between the EU and its Member States. It is through these relationships that the EU attempts to harmonise its policies in all areas. An interesting point to consider are the issues of prostitution and rape that, in most jurisdictions, are subject to strict criminal justice regulation. Criminal justice enforcement is one of the key markers of the sovereignty, or the legal authority, of the nation state. Today, however, we witness a shift in those power relationships as certain crimes are regulated at the supranational or EU levels (Ashworth & Zedner, 2014). Traditionally, the EU does not have legal

---

[4] Available at: https://www.theguardian.com/world/2020/jul/26/poland-withdraw-from-treaty-violence-against-women-istanbul-convention. Accessed 4 September 2020. See also: https://www.euronews.com/2021/04/01/istanbul-convention-poland-moves-a-step-closer-to-quitting-domestic-violence-treaty. Accessed 8 September 2021.

competencies on matters in these areas, but it applies its symbolic power to make political interventions which, in turn, may urge Member States to follow suit in their domestic laws. As European harmonisation moves into sexual politics, particularly in the case of prostitution and rape, it changes the relationship between the EU and the nation state both in how the EU brings issues around gender and sexuality under its remit (an area that is linked to national identity politics), and by taking responsibility for criminal justice responses (an area that is linked to national sovereignty) (Yuval-Davis, 1997). For now, the EU does not directly regulate how Member States address prostitution and rape but is it possible to identify new and emerging trends. We will discuss those trends in the chapters that follow.

Foucault defined genealogy as a method for analysing discourses as historically variable ways of creating power relationships through specifying knowledge and 'truth' (1980: 93). In this book, we invoke his method of analysis to examine not *who* holds power in European law and policy on gender and sexuality, but rather to think critically about *how* power is exercised through the interplay of discourses around gender and sexuality, and *how* this delimits or enables individuals' and groups' abilities to act in their interests. We apply this approach because it gives us the conceptual tools necessary to examine how this process operates from particular European nations' vantage points, and to interrogate that which the EU, national governments and other stakeholders have 'taken for granted or in the process of becoming fixed in the sense that their contested nature is forgotten' (Kutay, 2014: 4). For our purposes in this book, it is particularly pertinent to investigate how the EU has moved from regulating gender and sexuality issues related to the general labour market to addressing prostitution and rape and, thus, moving into spheres that are clearly both under domestic jurisdictions and are private matters.

To do this, we will probe how four EU Member States—Germany, Italy, Poland and Sweden–debate and respond to EU efforts to harmonise policies in these areas. We have chosen these jurisdictions because they are good case studies to highlight the issues at stake concerning the relationship between the EU's agenda and national agendas, and between the state and citizen in the area of sexual politics. The EU's attempts to harmonise its policies has been met with both praise and critique across the Union but often for different reasons. This draws attention to some interesting hierarchies and fault lines around social and cultural norms and values between different Member States around gender and sexuality.

Investigating the EU's desire for increased harmonisation on these particular issues can also provide us with key insights into contemporary debates and tensions relative to trends in the EU's competencies and its Member States' concerns over national sovereignty. Moreover, it is also important to note that how the issues of prostitution and rape enter the public imagination and circulate in civil society can prompt policy-makers to act. Ultimately, this may provide the EU with a stronger lever to further its role as a criminal justice institution, facilitate increased harmonisation and change what it considers EU policy fields and governance techniques.

Sexual Politics in Contemporary Europe addresses this topic in two interconnected ways. First, we use our unique feminist theoretical framework to examine EU and national disjuncture and conflict in this area. Two key concepts are core to our theoretical framework, namely that we can understand European sexual politics and the discourses and practices shaping it as both a *moving target* and a *sitting duck*. What do we mean by this, exactly? First, we argue that gender and sexuality are *moving targets*, in the sense that their meaning and function are changing in contemporary Europe and that this means that policy makers and citizens alike face challenges as they manoeuvre in a shifting discursive terrain. Secondly, and at a more applied level, we argue that the EU and national governments use these gender and sexuality norms and values to serve specific political and symbolic ends. Deploying these concepts in our analysis of the relationships between EU and Member States, we examine how prostitution and rape shift constantly between being mobile fields of meaning *moving targets* to becoming *sitting ducks* apt to be appropriated for politics around European identity, principles, cultural politics, citizenship and belonging.

Importantly, in our four case study countries, prostitution and rape are law and policy issues that are also linked to migration politics (Andrijasevic, 2003). In the case of rape, fears over gender norms and sexual practices among newly arrived migrants fuel heated debates around the need for stricter laws and criminal enforcement to protect 'us' from 'them' (Sjöberg & Sarwar, 2020). Similarly, the EU and its Member States conflate migration, human trafficking and prostitution, making it difficult to discuss prostitution separately from immigration, border control, law and order and 'modern-day sexual slavery' (Crowhurst & Skilbrei, 2018; FitzGerald, 2016). Related to the last point, in this book, we will interrogate what governments' attempts at balancing repressive and permissive policies, as well as punishment and rights, reveal about how they invoke law's expressive function. By this we mean: how governments and civil society actors use the law to affect behaviour beyond deterrence to realise social and normative change (Fox, 2013). We find that across the Union, national governments and various civil society actors invoke law's expressive function variously and for different reasons to problematise prostitution and rape in the service of issues of higher political importance.

Our analysis will also address how the EU uses discourses of gender and sexuality as leverage to regulate and inform its relationships with countries outside the EU. Seeing policy development around gender and sexuality as evolutionary not only misrepresents and depoliticises what is currently afoot in Europe, but also positions certain non-European 'Others' as lagging behind, as somehow less advanced (Kulpa & Mizielińska, 2011). Thus, the symbolic and political associations around discourses of gender 'norms' and sexual behaviours have also racialised and classed consequences because they shape how the EU promotes the 'correct' version of European values and identity 'at home', and in its relationships with geo-specific nations 'out there' (FitzGerald, 2010).

Drilling Down into European Norms and Values Around Gender and Sexuality

As we mentioned previously, one of the most important aspects of how the EU instrumentalises discourses of gender and sexuality occurs through its attempts to harmonise policies across the Union. At its inception, the EU was a platform for harmonising and protecting market conditions and labour in Europe. Over time, it expanded its competencies and aimed to establish common European institutions and norms to encompass most policy areas (Knill & Preidel, 2015). For example, and as we discuss in Chapter 2, when the Treaty of Amsterdam (EC 1997) entered into force in 1999, the EU acknowledged gender equality as a 'common European value'. A decade later, it made standards for policies on 'sexual orientation' pan-European principles. Thus, we observe a direct correlation between gender and sexuality discourses on the one hand, and how the EU has intervened strategically on policy issues on the other. This is particularly important given that, until recently, the EU has considered many of these policy areas matters for domestic legal regimes to address because they were outside EU competence.

As the EU takes a firmer hand in soft law policy decisions and values statements around gender and sexuality, we find that it is necessary to intervene and pose the following question: What is the nature of the European policy realm around gender and sexuality?

In an attempt to begin to answer this question, throughout this book we use publicly available primary data to answer this question. Soft law policies such as voluntary Resolutions are not the only means available to the EU to harmonise how European states approach their problems. EU law and the European Court of Justice (CJEU) offer other alternatives. Currently, and as we will outline in more detail in Chapter 2, the Treaty of Lisbon (TFEU 2007)[5] defines the relationship between EU institutions. When the Treaty came into force in 2009, the EU acquired competence in criminal procedure and gained substantive legal powers. In concrete terms that are particularly relevant to this book's themes, this gave the European Commission (hereafter the Commission) the legal scope to attempt to harmonise minimum standards for certain crimes or 'Euro-crimes' defined thus because Article 83(1) TFEU identifies them as transborder offences. For example, the EU tackles human trafficking and sexual exploitation of women and children as among the ten Euro-crimes regulated by EU law. The challenge for the EU as it attempts to achieve full EU harmonisation around gender and sexuality policies and procedures is that most of the related crimes do not come under EU jurisdiction.

While the EU has a narrow jurisdiction, it has been able to widen its regulatory net by convincing Member States that particular legislation advances the 'European' project in how it expresses and builds social norms. Importantly, these frameworks establish best practices around welfare and criminal justice for all Member States, and form part of the 'Copenhagen Criteria'[6] that proscribe the rules to determine aspiring Member States' eligibility for EU membership. Furthermore, the EU's territorial and extra-territorial disciplining power that it applies through its development aid, for example, has the power to compel states outside the EU's jurisdiction to change their legislation and policies in order to become more 'European' (FitzGerald, 2012). In Foucault's (2000) terms, governmentality and biopolitical regulation on this scale give the

---

[5] Available at: https://eur-lex.europa.eu/legal-content/EN/TXT/?uri=OJ:C:2007:306:TOC. Accessed 8 September 2020.

[6] Available at: https://ec.europa.eu/neighbourhood-enlargement/policy/glossary/terms/accession-criteria_en. Accessed 2 July 2020.

EU leverage in its relationships with its Member States and other nations. Entry into the EU is conditioned on prospective members' ability to align their domestic law and policy with EU gender equality norms. Furthermore and as part of this process, they need to demonstrate their commitment to combat violence against women (VAW) via soft law policies (Montoya, 2013).

Just as important as what the EU determines are European legal norms and values around gender and sexuality, is what it determines to be alien to notions of Europeanness (FitzGerald, 2010). Historians have described how the meaning and practice of gender and sexuality norms in various European contexts have shifted over time (Herzog, 2011). We can trace this to the roles that gender and sexuality have played in European policy developments in the late 1990s as ideals around European identities and citizenship have pivoted towards sex-related concerns such as gender, sexual citizenship and intimate life (Herzog, 2011). A good example of this is Europe's preoccupation with Islam and its associated practices of gender and sexual repression. This issue has created surprising political and ideological alignments among what would otherwise be diametrically opposed political factions. For example, it has enabled conservative European forces to rally around and promote 'tolerance' on gender and sexuality affairs as a European value (Butler, 2009; Gressgård & Jacobsen, 2008). Although 'tolerance' of difference is a central reference point for the EU's version of 'Europeanness', being 'intolerant' of certain cultural practices such as female genital mutilation (FGM) is also a necessary expression of said 'Europeanness'.

Alongside a discussion of discourses of tolerance and rejection of VAW as key European traits, it is equally important to consider the power structures and regulatory techniques that underpin and support this discursive framework and to understand whose interests they serve (Josephson, 2016). Central to this argument is the view that the inclusions/exclusions made on the basis of gender and sexuality reveal something important about how Europeans negotiate their identities. This takes on more importance at the institutional level when such discourses lead to policies that define what is 'in place'/'out of place' in the European body politic (FitzGerald, 2010).

Viewed through the lens of protection, law is a normative technology that can be used to include or exclude, equalise or differentiate. Researchers have noted that establishing a European identity and collective reactivates and redeploys radicalised and gendered discourses about

Europe's significant 'Others', and that sexuality plays an important role in this (Baer, 2002).[7] Fears about the 'Other's' sexuality emerge as contributing to creating 'imagined communities', to use Anderson's (1991) phrase. In contemporary European sexual politics, the intersection of categories of 'race', gender and sexuality are never far from political debate.

This brings us to the centre ground of European regulatory policies that shape lives and identities, and the processes of inclusion/exclusion that have evolved to uphold and defend a hegemonic version of European citizenship. When feminists began to critique the hegemonic citizenship model, they did so by challenging the historic doctrine of separate spheres (Davidoff & Hall, 1987). This 'naturalisation' of the socio-spatial separation of the sexes with two sets of norms and values reached its ultimate expression in the seventeenth century with the rise of capitalism. Western societies segregated production and consumption, with the latter confined to a reconceptualised notion of the family, especially the bourgeois family. The European middle classes differentiated between a 'masculine' public world of production, civic and intellectual life, and 'feminine' private spaces of home, hearth and reproduction (Nicholson, 1994). Feminists argued that this artificial divide was important in the continued subordination of women's citizenship rights up to the latter half of the twentieth-century (Mouffe, 1995; Pateman, 1989). For example, they challenged the 'harm principle' stemming from John Stuart Mill's (1859) liberal moral and political philosophy, which asserted that the state could only exercise its power over a citizen to prevent or punish serious harm to others (Scoular & FitzGerald, 2021). Accordingly, the 'private' realm must be free from government influence and other social institutions. Feminists and others argued that the protection of the 'private' as a sphere of non-intervention was a dangerous ideology that legitimated ignoring many injustices, including VAW as 'just' domestic violence (Edwards, 1989). Feminism has made significant incursions in problematising what counts as the 'private' and the 'political' by reasoning that certain problems are not essentially personal but societal and, therefore, something law and policy should address (Fraser, 2010; Young, 1990).

This brings us to recent developments in feminist thinking around citizenship in contemporary Europe, which are shaped by two key frames.

---

[7] 'Others' does not refer here to real persons, but rather to an abstract and fetishised representation of danger and 'the outside' (see e.g. Ahmed, 2000).

The first concerns social rights relative to neoliberal challenges to the welfare state. The second concerns reproductive, sexual and cultural rights (Lister et al., 2007). A consequent effect of these challenges to the dominant model for citizenship is that it has produced new formulations of citizenship, such as 'intimate citizenship' and 'cultural citizenship' (Stevenson, 2003: 331).

Membership of the polity, however, is not just a question of rights and obligations. It includes also a range of social and political relationships, practices and identities that combined, produce what we might call 'belonging'. The key to belonging is participation. Fraser identifies 'parity of participation' or the right to resources and access to public political space 'to interact with one another as peers' as key to democratic citizenship (2010: 16). These insights have been influential and form an important counterpoint to the dominant feminist model of citizenship. They have also provided a theoretical position, from which it becomes possible to 'rethink' how we could analyse how regulatory policies support supranational, national and cultural understandings of citizenship *vis-à-vis* those bodies and practices deemed to be 'sexual strangers' (Phelan, 2001: 11) and how this occurs via restrictive and hegemonic notions of democratic citizenship (Pateman, 1989).

This is the very point where we raise the notion of 'sexual citizenship' (Josephson, 2016; Plummer, 2003; Stychin, 2003) to work in this book. Simply put: the concept serves as another conceptual resource for an analysis and critique of what proponents argue is a paternalistic form of state-centric systems of inclusion/exclusion based on the principle of good/bad sexual citizens. Thus, sexual citizenship articulates both 'sexual rights claims and promotes the citizenship status of groups whose sexuality is stigmatised' (Lister et al., 2007: 9). This line of thinking has inspired our work in this book. It serves as a framing device that challenges us to turn our analytical lens around, and to think through how the desire to defend and prioritise a particular vision of gender and sexual identities and practices serves the interests of the powerful (Josephson, 2016). With these thoughts in mind, we structure this book as follows.

Chapter 2 provides the reader with a contextual framework for our analysis of European sexual politics. It aims to unravel and clarify the discourses, processes, actors and institutions operating in this discursive space at the EU and national levels. The chapter takes a historical perspective to contextualise European sexual politics through an elaboration of how the EU has, over time, chosen to include some issues as relevant to the European project and its goals, and exclude others. We will map the history of the EU's gender equality *acquis*—all the enforceable and legally binding Treaties and Directives. Specifically, we will map the EU's gradual expansion from conceptualising gender equality as an economic imperative to a broad goal of integrating the principle of equal treatment through law in all EU policy areas. This discussion will also include a consideration of how the EU deploys its soft law policies—Resolutions, Recommendations, Communications, positive action measures—to ensure the principle of equal impact for all through gender mainstreaming.

Following this, we take up Foucault's method of genealogy to trace 'the constitution of knowledges, discourses, domains' (1980: 117) in two specific EU policy areas; namely, prostitution and rape. To do this we pose two interrelated questions, namely: (1) How is the EU harmonising its policies in such cases and (2) To what effect? By focussing on European sexual politics as dynamic and relational processes, we hope to offer a more nuanced account of how discourses of gender and sexuality coalesce around and contribute to how the EU works today. In this way, *Sexual Politics in Contemporary Europe* provides the first theoretical steps in what we hope will be a wider conversation around how gender and sexuality politics contribute to the trajectory and contemporary predicament of 'the European project'.

Chapters 3 and 4 comprise two interrelated policy areas, which illuminate critical elements of the EU's attempts to harmonise European social and legal norms around prostitution and rape. These policies foreground different aspects of how the EU makes, communicates and transposes its norms and values around gender and sexuality around the Union. Both prostitution and rape laws have traditionally fallen within the remit of domestic legal regimes and nation states' normative discussions and developments. Recently, however, the EU has taken a more active interest in them as policy issues. These policy domains serve as examples of what happens when the EU extends its interests and investments in other policy fields to ensure that its Member States integrate its desired norms and values into their domestic policy.

Using our feminist theoretical framework, Chapter 3 begins by offering an historical perspective on prostitution regulation in Europe. Specifically, we wish to contextualise the trajectory of European prostitution law and policy. Then, the chapter elaborates on contemporary approaches to prostitution regulation. It explores why and how Sweden became the first jurisdiction in the world to unilaterally criminalise sex purchase. The chapter explores how, at the EU level, feminist lobbyists draw their argumentation, legitimacy and content for their policy proposals from Sweden by stating that Sweden's experiences are so positive that the whole Union ought to follow suit. The chapter concludes by examining the feminist debates at the EU level that have led to the European Parliament (hereafter EP) adopting a policy stance that, for the first time, institutionalises a European approach to prostitution via an EP Resolution on *sexual exploitation and prostitution and its impact on gender equality*.[8]

Chapter 4 turns to the contemporary 'moment' in sexual politics around rape and other forms of sexual violence in Europe. We are interested not in how the EU and its Member States regulate rape per se, but rather in how rape 'emerges as a target for government' (Rose & Valverde, 1998). Using Foucault's theory of governmentality as the 'conduct of conduct' and integrating it into our theoretical framework, we interrogate the tensions and conflicts surrounding the EU's attempts to harmonise norms and values with the express purpose of achieving 'an ever closer union' between Member States as expressed in the Treaty of Rome (EEC 1957). We examine how, as the EU attempts to push for harmonisation across the Union, rape as a gender equality issue to becomes both a *moving target* and a *sitting duck* entwined in EU and domestic level politics. We divide this chapter into three sections. In Section One entitled: 'Positioning Rape in the EU Political Imaginary', we situate the current 'moment' in feminist thinking around VAW generally, and around sexual violence in particular, at the EU level. In Section Two entitled: 'Establishing 'a European' Position on VAW', we drill down into why and how rape have become implicated in the EU's desire for 'ever closer union'. Finally, in Section Three entitled: 'The EU's Hard and Soft Approach to VAW', we map the EU hard and soft law policies on rape.

Acting as a conduit between Chapters 3 and 4, Chapter 5 combines the issues of prostitution and rape by outlining how four Member States adopt or resist EU policy recommendations in this area. These countries have different histories as EU members. For example, both (West) Germany and Italy were among the EU's founding members. Sweden

[8] Available at: https://www.europarl.europa.eu/doceo/document/TA-7-2014-0162_EN.html. Accessed 24 April 2021.

joined in 1995 and Poland was one of the ten countries included in the EU's expansion eastward in 2004. Furthermore, the four case studies relate differently to the EU as a platform to realise national goals and legitimacy. At one end of the scale is Sweden, which seems to treat the EU as a venue to 'spread the gospel' about the benefits and successes of 'going Swedish' across all policy areas. Then, at the other end of the scale is Poland, which seems to be constantly embattled in internal and international conflicts over its relationship with the EU. In this national context, far right politics invoke discourses of 'European values' around gender and sexuality as proxies to argue that they are the vanguard who are, in fact, protecting national catholic values (Kulpa & Mizielińska, 2016). By contrast, Brussels frames these activities as 'backward' and emblematic of the threat posed by traditionalism to the European project (Graff, 2014; Konopka et al., 2020).

And finally, in Chapter 6, we offer a brief conclusion which reflects upon the current situation and the challenges the EU faces when making gender and sexuality its business.

References

Ahmed, S. (2000). *Strange encounters embodied others in post-coloniality.* Routledge.

Anderson, B. (1991). *Imagined communities: Reflections on the origin and spread of nationalism.* Verso Books.

Andrijasevic, R. (2003). The difference borders make: (Il)legality, migration and trafficking in Italy among Eastern European women in prostitution. In S. Ahmed, C. Castaneda, A. M. Fortier, & M. Sheller (Eds.), *Uprootings/Regroundings: Questions of home and migration* (pp. 251–272). Berg.

Ashworth, A., & Zedner, L. (2014). *The historical origins of a preventive state.* Oxford University Press.

Baer, B. 2002. Russian gays/Western gaze: Mapping (homo)sexual desire in post-Soviet Russia. *GLQ: A Journal of Lesbian and Gay Studies,* 8(4), 499–521.

Bell, D., & Binne, J. (2000). *The sexual citizen: Queer politics and beyond.* Wiley.

Butler, J. (2009). *Intimate citizenship: Gender, sexualities, politics.* Routledge.

Crowhurst, I., & Skilbrei, M.-L. (2018). International comparative explorations of prostitution policies: Lessons from two European projects. *Innovation: The European Journal of Social Science Research,* 3(2), 142–161.

Davidoff, L., & Hall, C. (1987). *Family fortunes: Men and women of the English middle class 1780–1850.* Routledge.

Dunphy, R. (2000). *Sexual politics. An introduction.* Edinburgh University Press.

Edwards, S. (1989). *Policing domestic violence: Women, the law and the state*. Sage.

Euchner, E. (2019). *Morality politics in a secular age: Strategic parties and divided governments*. Palgrave Macmillan.

FitzGerald, S. (2010). Biopolitics and the regulation of vulnerability: The case of the female trafficked migrant. *International Journal of Law in Context*, 6(3), 277–294.

FitzGerald, S. (2012). Vulnerable bodies, vulnerable borders: Extraterritoriality and human trafficking. *Feminist Legal Studies*, 20(3), 227–244.

FitzGerald, S. (2016). Vulnerable geographies: Human trafficking, immigration and border control in the UK and beyond. *Gender, Place & Culture*, 23(2), 181–197.

Foucault, M. (1980). *The history of sexuality: Volume one: An introduction*. Vintage Books.

Foucault, M. (2000). *Power: Essential works of Foucault, 1954–1984*. Penguin.

Fox, M. (2013). Feminist perspectives on theories of punishment: Feminist-perspectives on criminal law. In D. Nicholson & L. Bibbings (Eds.), *Feminist perspectives on criminal law* (pp. 79–100). Routledge-Cavendish.

Fraser, N. (2010). *The scales of justice: Reimagining political space in a globalising world*. Columbia University Press.

Graff, A. (2014). Report from the gender trenches: War against 'genderism' in Poland. *European Journal of Women's Studies*, 21(4), 431–435.

Gressgård, R., & Jacobsen, C. M. (2008). Krevende toleranse: Islam og homoseksualitet. *Tidsskrift for Kjønnsforskning*, 3(2), 22–39.

Herzog, D. (2011). *Sexuality in Europe: A twentieth-century history: New approaches to European history*. Cambridge University Press.

Josephson, J. (2016). *Rethinking sexual citizenship*. SUNY Press.

Knill, C., & Preidel, C. (2015). Institutional opportunity structures and the Catholic Church: Explaining variation in the regulation of same-sex partnerships in Ireland and Italy. *Journal of European Public Policy*, 2(3), 374–390.

Konopka, K., Prusik, M., & Szulawski, M. (2020). Two sexes, two genders only: Measuring attitudes toward transgender individuals in Poland. *Sex Roles*, 82(9), 600–621.

Kulpa, R., & Mizielińska, J. (2011). *De-centring westerns sexualities: Central and Eastern European perspectives*. Routledge.

Kulpa, R., & Mizielinska, J. (eds.) (2016). *De-centring western sexualities: Central and Eastern European perspectives*. London: Routledge.

Kutay, A. (2014). *Governance and European civil society: Governmentality, discourse and NGOs*. Routledge.

Locher, B., & Prügl, E. (2009). Gender perspectives. In *European integration theory* (pp. 181–198). Oxford University Press.

Le Roux, E. (2017). Faith-based HIV response in post-Soviet Eastern Europe: The case of Channels of Hope in Russia, Romania, and Armenia. *Development in Practice, 27*(5), 658–669.

Lister, R., Williams, F., Anttonen, A., Gerhard, U., & Bussemaker, J. (2007). *Gendering citizenship in Western Europe: New challenges for citizenship research in a cross-national context*. Policy Press.

Mattson, G. (2015). Style and the value of gay nightlife: Homonormative placemaking in San Francisco. *Urban Studies, 5*(16), 3144–3159.

Mepschen, P., & Duyvendak, J. (2012). European sexual nationalisms: The culturalisation of citizenship and the sexual politics of belonging and exclusion. *Perspectives on Europe, 42*(1), 70–76.

Mills, J. S. (1859). *On Liberty*. London: John W. Parker and Son.

Montoya, C. (2013). *From global to grassroots: The European Union, transnational advocacy, and combating violence against women*. Oxford University Press.

Mouffe, C. (1995). Politics, democratic action, and solidarity. *Inquiry, 38*(1–2), 99–108.

Nicholson, L. (1994). Interpreting gender. *Signs, 20*(1), 79–105.

Pateman, C. (1989). *The disorder of women: Democracy, feminism, and political theory*. Stanford University Press.

Paternotte, D., & Kuhar, R. (2017). "Gender ideology" in movement: Introduction. In R. Kuhar & D. Paternotte (Eds.), *Anti-gender campaigns in Europe: Mobilising against equality* (pp. 1–22). Rowman & Littlefield.

Phelan, S. (2001). *Sexual strangers: Gays, lesbians, and dilemmas of citizenship*. Temple University Press.

Plummer, K. (2003). *Intimate citizenship: Private decisions and public dialogues*. University of Washington Press.

Rose, N., & Valverde, M. (1998). Governed by law? *Social & Legal Studies, 7*(4), 541–551.

Scoular, J., & FitzGerald, S. (2021). Why decriminalise prostitution? Because law and justice aren't always the same. *International Journal for Crime, Justice and Social Democracy, 19*(4): 56–64. https://doi.org/10.5204/ijcsd.1996

Sjöberg, M., & Sarwar, F. (2020). Who gets blamed for rapes: Effects of immigration status on the attribution of blame toward victims and perpetrators. *Journal of Interpersonal Violence, 35*(3–14), 2446–2463.

Stevenson, N. (2003). Cultural citizenship in the 'cultural society': A cosmopolitan approach. *Citizenship Studies, 7*(3), 331–348.

Stychin, C. (2003). *Governing sexuality: The changing politics of citizenship and law reform*. Hart Publishing.

Vance, C. (1992). *Pleasure and danger: Exploring female sexuality* (2nd ed.). Routledge.

Weeks, J. (2012). *Sex, politics and society: The regulations of sexuality since 1800* (3rd ed.). Routledge.

Young, I. (1990). *Justice and the politics of difference*. Princeton University Press.

Yuval-Davis, N. (1997). *Gender and nation*. Sage.

CHAPTER 2

On the Road to Lisbon: Europe Becoming a Normative Community

Abstract This chapter traces how Europe addresses gender and sexuality as issues central to the EU's harmonisation agenda. It maps the contours of EU policy-making around gender and sexuality and illuminates a series of paradoxes and tensions that render them a *moving target* and a *sitting duck* in European sexual politics. Our approach raises questions about how gender and sexuality are inextricably linked to conflicts around the meaning of gender and sexuality, and to how the EU and its Member States take up those meanings in conflicts over a normative European identity at the EU level versus national identity politics at the Member State level. The chapter examines the issues that brought gender and sexuality under EU law and policy remit, how this change in EU policy priorities have become possible and why certain Member States accept or resist these changes. The chapter is structured around three interconnected themes, (1) the EU's strategy around harmonisation, (2) EU policy processes and (3) the role of civil society actors in EU policy-making in the area of gender and sexuality.

Keywords Harmonisation · Normative identity · Europeanness · National identity politics · Civil society

© The Author(s), under exclusive license to Springer Nature Switzerland AG 2022
S. FitzGerald and M.-L. Skilbrei, *Sexual Politics in Contemporary Europe*,
https://doi.org/10.1007/978-3-030-91174-4_2

The discursive arc surrounding the meaning of the EU's gender and sexuality politics is complex and layered. This requires that we approach it in terms of a 'polity' (i.e., its institutions and structure), its 'policy framework' (i.e., the measures it develops and applies) and its 'politics' (i.e., the ways in which policy-making occurs as a result of allegiances, bargaining and dominance) (Diez & Wiener, 2009: 18–19). This approach sets up this chapter's central concerns, which aim to trace how Europe addresses gender and sexuality as issues central to the EU's harmonisation agenda. While it is beyond the book's scope to delve into all EU policy interests in this area, we aim to provide the reader with a conceptual map that assembles in miniature two of the key thematic areas of European law and policymaking relevant to our focus. By charting the contours of EU policymaking around gender and sexuality, we will illuminate a series of paradoxes and tensions that render them both *moving targets* and *sitting ducks* in European sexual politics. Our approach raises questions about how gender and sexuality are inextricably linked to conflicts around the meaning of gender and sexuality, and how the EU and its Member States take up those meanings in conflicts over a normative European identity at the EU level versus national identity politics at the Member State level. This focus necessitates that we examine the issues that have brought gender and sexuality under the EU's law and policy remit, how this change in EU policy priorities has become possible and why certain Member States accept or resist these changes. We divide this chapter into three interconnected sections in order to manage and communicate effectively these complex relationships. In Section One entitled: 'Establishing an Ever Closer Union Among the People of Europe' of the chapter, we explore the EU's strategy around harmonisation. In Section Two entitled: 'How Can We Understand European Policy Processes Around Gender and Sexuality?' of the chapter, we explore EU policy processes. In the final part of the chapter, we examine the role of civil society actors in EU policymaking in the area of gender and sexuality.

Establishing an Ever Closer Union Among the People of Europe

It is not possible to talk about how the EU attempts to harmonise gender and sexuality discourses without first being clear about why and how the EU has brought them within its law and policy remit. In the context of this book, this requires an analysis that addresses the EU's attempts to harmonise norms and values across the Union. We begin, therefore, by mapping the EU legal framework relative to our areas of interest.

Treaties are the EU's overarching legal framework for advancing its political agenda. It is via these treaties that it establishes its remit for binding and non-binding instruments that govern Member States' activities in specific areas. Heads of state or governments sign treaties. Once signed, these treaties establish the areas in which the EU can engage politically and legally. Article 288 of the Treaty of Lisbon (TFEU 2007) establishes that the EU can issue legal acts including Regulations, Directives, Decisions, Recommendations and Opinions, where all but the last two are binding for Member States (Borchardt, 2017). Over time, the EU has developed a broad range of instruments that we can divide into 'hard law', 'soft law polices' and non-legal norms (Beveridge, 2012). The categories are important in the context of this book because the EU defines soft law policy as a policy that does not instruct Member States in their law-making, but rather it denotes those policies where non-compliance will result in legal consequences for Member States (Beveridge, 2012). For the purpose of this book, we will distinguish between hard law (direct and coercive strategies) and soft law policy (indirect normative strategies). Both have practical effects and Member States' failure to follow them will have ramifications for them. Furthermore, we recognise both as stemming from the same political rationality but they are rooted in different governmental technologies (Rose & Miller, 1992).

The EU considers the Treaty of Rome (EEC 1957) as its founding document. The Preamble to the Treaty contains the Community's objective, which is to lay the foundations of 'an ever closer union among the peoples of Europe'. The EU identifies this spirit of greater union as the principle that binds its members together. At its inception, the Treaty established the rules of formation for a European common market. It became a means of creating gradual harmonisation on particular issues, such as trade. Importantly, particularly in terms of our interests in the volume, Article 119 EEC (what is now Article 157 TFEU) established the legal basis for the early harmonisation of the principle of gender equality in Europe through the principle of equal pay between women and men for equal work (Ahrens, 2019). Although Member States should have transposed Article 119 EEC into their domestic laws by 1962, many were unwilling or unable to do so. Critics observe that this has established a pattern that continues to this day around how the EU and its Member States view and instrumentalise the principle of gender equality as 'grounded in market rationalities' (Guerrina, 2020: 128). It is worth noting that because gender equality remains a contested issue in the relationship between the EU and certain Member States, and this is something to which we will return to frequently through this volume, the Treaty states also that the EU will create *other* joint policies *if* required.

By the 1970s and against a backdrop of social upheaval, high unemployment and industrial action in Europe, the EU concentrated on welfare-oriented harmonisation in its policies. It sought to expand the protection of women beyond the issue of equal pay for equal work with the establishment of three Directives (Mazey, 1998). Allied to this, the Paris Summit in 1972 established that the EU should move beyond regulating trade and economic life. Furthermore in 1974, the EU established its Social Action Programme. From this, EU involvement in gender equality expanded through extension of its competencies. And yet, it would be a mistake to interpret these initiatives as a celebration of gender equality in all its forms. Rather, as the Directives suggest, the concept of gender equality continues to function in policy in a way that enables the EU to respond to its and its the Member States' desire for increased labour mobility across the Union by strengthening workers' rights in the European labour market (Jacquot, 2015). Since the Treaty of Rome included provisions to address those areas where workers might be subjected to harm and exploitation in jurisdictions where they were not citizens, the EU's obligations began to evolve from merely facilitating market forces to protecting people from it (Kantola, 2010).

Although the EU made little headway in the area of gender equality policy in the 1980s, it continued to develop its objective of ever closer union through a series of Declarations and Treaties. It was not, however, until the EU introduced the Treaty of Maastricht (TEU 1992) that it developed further the protection of gender equality through its adoption of 'the Social Protocol'. Crucially, the Treaty places an obligation on Member States to recognise that women and men are different and it is, therefore, necessary that they include measures in domestic law and policy to ensure gender equality. Another important feature is that the Treaty identifies equality between women and men as one of the common values on which the Union is founded (Article 2 TEU). Critics note that the consequent effect of this framing is that it continues to advance the EU's economic agenda by continuing to understand gender equality in economic terms. In this way, EU institutions appropriated feminist goals and rationalities to serve other policy aims, such as economic prosperity (Roseneil et al., 2012).

When the Treaty of Amsterdam (EC 1997) entered into force in 1999, Article 2 of the treaty widened and revised the concept of substantive gender equality to encompass one of the 'tasks of the Community'. Moreover, Article 3(2) of the treaty imposed an obligation of gender mainstreaming on the EU and its Member States for the first time. Gender mainstreaming refers to a deliberate soft law policy strategy that integrates a gender dimension in all policy areas rather than making gender a distinct policy area. In practice, this requires that the European legislator consider the principle of gender equality when drafting and implementing all legislation (Article 3 EC). Thus, the Treaty has empowered the EU to take positive action measures to address discrimination in several intersecting areas, including gender and sexuality, beyond the area of paid labour (MacRae & Weiner, 2017). With the mainstreaming of this obligation, the EU's competency assumed a social dimension in national institutions in Member States. Moreover, it transformed their obligations beyond considering gender equality as being a European value to being a Europe goal and *demanded* that Member States act to achieve it.

There is a similar logic at play within EU hard law. The Treaty of Lisbon (TFEU 2007) widened the EU gender equality *acquis* in two important and interconnected ways. First, it enhanced the European Parliament's (EP) legislative powers that established parity between it and the Council of the European Union (hereafter the Council) (Jacquot, 2015). Secondly, and because of this, the Treaty gave the Charter of Fundamental Rights (2000) 'the same legal value as the Treaties' (Article 6(1) TEU). Consequently, when the Treaty entered into force in 2009, the Charter acquired a legally binding character. In this book, we concentrate upon how the Charter establishes rights and obligations in key areas that are relevant to our interests. For example, Article 21(1) of the Charter prohibits discrimination 'based on sex, racial or ethnic origin, religion or belief, disability, age or sexual orientation'. The Charter's regulatory function of promoting and solidifying a European identity interests us also; on the one hand, because the Charter is the EU's de facto human rights instrument, but also on the other hand because the Charter provides the EU with 'a yardstick for determining whether a European State can be a candidate for *accession*, in accordance with Article 49 TEU' (Burri & Prechal, 2008: 5). Therefore, it serves an important function in the EU's plans for increased harmonisation.

While the EU's hard law provisions in this area 'protect' EU citizens' equality rights, what the EU's expansion of its legal framework means in practice for its ability to expand the EU project territorially and ideologically is a recurring theme in this book. For example, Article 83(1) of the Treaty of Lisbon (TFEU 2007) establishes minimum standards for criminal justice for Member States in specific areas such as security. As we mentioned previously, Article 83(1) of the Treaty states that the EU can harmonise substantive criminal law to regulate 'Euro-crimes' or 'offences which…deserve to be dealt with at the EU level because of their particularly serious nature and their cross border dimension'. This prompts us to pose the following question: How is this relevant to our objectives in this book? In short, the answer is that it is central. Article 83(1) TFEU establishes minimum rules for the offence of 'trafficking in human beings *and* sexual exploitation of women and children'.[1] Therefore, this normative agenda highlights how gender and sexuality interact with EU level politics as *moving targets* to establish a European understanding and meaning of gender equality, while simultaneously serving as free-floating discourse or *sitting duck* that the EU, its institutions and other actors can deploy variously in areas beyond gender justice such as securitisation, border and immigration control and crime.

Here is an apt moment to raise the issue of the role that feminists working in EU institutions, such as the EP, play in framing which topics the EU takes up as Euro-crimes, how this process occurs and the meaning those issues take on at the centres of EU power and decision-making. The EP has typically been an early responder to gender and sexuality policy demands, stemming from civil society actors representing politically marginalised populations in this forum (Liebert, 2003). Thus, having a presence in Parliamentary committees, for example, enhances civil society actors' abilities to push certain issues onto the EU agenda (Allwood, 2018). Put simply, it enables them to participate in the work of agenda-setting by making issues both *moving targets* and *sitting ducks* in EU level deliberations.

Commentators observe that this process of gaining access to political space and participating in agenda-setting is one of the ways, in which feminists participate in the 'Europeanisation of public discourses'

---

[1] Emphasis added.

(Kantola, 2010: 209). Moreover, as certain issues assume a more prominent position on the EU agenda, and as discourses around these issues assume normative status, it becomes increasingly difficult for more marginal civil society actors, such as sex worker activists or migrant groups, to participate as equals in this political space (FitzGerald & Freedman, 2021). Thus, establishing a social norm around what is the meaning of gender equality in the area of prostitution, for example, can be as effective in its disciplining power to act upon people across the Union as the law, following Foucault (1977). This is Scoular's (2010) point when she critiques feminist scholars who conclude that law is irrelevant for the operation of sex markets because they cannot find evidence for how law has influenced those markets' size and composition directly. Scoular argues that this interpretation builds upon an outmoded idea of law. She contends that law is most appropriately examined as one of several regulatory mechanisms that normalise particular ways of feeling (affect) and particular ways of being (personhood).

We will return to this issue in more detail below through a discussion of how radical feminist inspired neo-abolitionists working within EU committees have been at the forefront of frame-setting in this area (Allwood, 2018; FitzGerald & Freedman, 2021). For now, it is sufficient to note that Swedish feminist thinking around the connection between prostitution, sex trafficking and gender equality has been instrumental in shaping feminist thinking in EU institutions in what Woodward (2004) defines as the velvet triangle. In short, the velvet triangle is a heuristic concept to describe interactions between policymakers and politicians, feminist academics and experts in the EU policy sphere. By conflating prostitution and sex trafficking, the velvet triangle has been able to link issues around gender and sexuality in ways that have transformed human trafficking into a Euro-crime and, in the process, it has implicated prostitution as an attendant issue. In this, we see further evidence of how ideas and mechanisms for the control and regulation of gender and sexuality in Europe function in the service of issues of higher political importance. As this point is key to our analysis, we want to interrogate it relative to the harmonisation process at the EU level.

What Europe's political climate regarding gender and sexuality illustrates is that it is not a given that the policy shifts that have been introduced via EU treaties will automatically lead to more gender equality or rights for women or sexual minorities in Member States. Since gender and sexuality norms vary across the Union, this means that enforcing policy alignment alone will not suffice in harmonising the treaties.

Of course, the on-the-ground reality is that some countries are already ahead of the EU in their ability to institutionalise gender equality ideology. Consequently, they function as the gold standard against which the EU models its future policy. This, in turn, contributes to creating a hierarchy of Europeanness among EU Member States. For example, we see this when certain Northern European countries view Southern and Eastern European countries as consistently lagging behind 'best practice' (Dzenovska, 2018). As the EU strengthens its ambition to be a unified normative community, it runs the risk, in certain quarters, of being negatively construed as a 'civilising project'. On this question, Butler points to how 'Europe has claimed ownership not only of what is good and rational, but also over what is progressive and radical' (2009: 17). An aspect of this is that notions of Europeanness remain racialised. Commentators from outside the EU recognise how 'European' has come to stand for 'good' and 'civilized'; a phenomenon described by Blagojevic (2011) in her analysis of Serbian popular resistance to achieving EU integration through normative alignment.

Similarly within the EU, there have been several incidents where the EU deems national laws and practices to be in breach of European values. Critics have described the EU's desire for greater harmonisation in law and policy as losing sight of Member States' different legal norms, economic resources, policing cultures and gender relations. Therefore, they point to the challenges these nations face as they attempt to implement policies designed for other jurisdictions (Skilbrei, 2019). For example, Kamenou (2011) described how, in the case of Cyprus, the Orthodox Church opposed the national political ambition to align with European values and regulations around homosexuality. In this instance, the Church portrayed this alignment as undermining national interests and identities by 'Europeanising' the country. We find that this observation makes our point well: to reject what is considered European indicates how the individual nation imagines itself *vis-à-vis* Europe. It indicates also how gender and sexuality are implicated in that process. What is important to note is that when certain Member States accede to the EU and agree to abide by European norms and values, often they do so with a degree of ambivalence and caution. Szulc (2011) describes this situation when he points out that in modern-day Poland, certain factions associate sexual minorities with European decadence and degeneration.

In 2020, up to 100 local authorities in Poland declared themselves to be free of so-called LGBTQI ideology as gay rights became a high-profile issue domestically and internationally. Later in March 2021, Poland banned same-sex couples from adopting children. In a similar demonstration of resistance in June 2021, Hungary introduced a law that established a number of restrictive and discriminatory measures against acts that promoted 'divergence from self-identity corresponding to sex at birth, sex change or homosexuality' for individuals under the age of 18. In both cases, this set these Member States on a collision course with the EU over their violation of the principles of 'human dignity', 'freedom of expression and information', 'the right to respect of private life' and the 'right to non-discrimination' as enshrined in Articles 1, 7, 11 and 21 of the EU Charter of Fundamental Rights (2009). Finally, due to the severity of these violations, Poland and Hungary remain in direct violation of the values set down in Article 2 of the Treaty of Maastricht (TEU 1992). In Europe's current political climate, it seems that these Member States view their refusal to adopt and uphold EU values around gender and sexuality norms as a 'badge of honour' (Adler-Nissen, 2014: 144), against the encroachment of, as in the case of Hungary, 'nation's constitutional identity and values based on our Christian culture'.

How Can We Understand European Policy Processes Around Gender and Sexuality?

There is a large literature on how policies are made and implemented within the EU, in among other things the literature on Europeanisation (Radaelli, 2004). While our contribution is not to this literature per se, we do address the question of the dynamism of the relationship between EU and its Member States. Key in scholarly debates in this area is how one can understand the relationship between EU level bodies and Member States, not least the direction influences take as ideas are transposed 'upstream' from Member States via governmental and civil society engagement with EU bodies and decision-making processes, and 'downstream' via Europeanisation processes (Bulmer et al., 2009).

We submit that it is useful to understand the EU as a governance structure rather than an institution that governs its Member States. As such, it impacts developments through diverse instruments and within a network of actors that are both private and public operating at both the EU and national levels (Öhlén & Silander, 2020: 23). This means that the relationship between the EU and Member States is highly dependent on how compatible EU rules and institutions are with those of nation states (Öhlén & Silander, 2020: 21). Influencing EU's positions and ways of working is, thus, something that reduces friction between governance levels.

As the EU has become more invested in social policies that move it beyond regulating market relations, its patterns of the application of policy instruments have changed. Maj (2014) pointed to how in the 1980s the EU introduced Resolutions and other soft law policies to replace harder measures, and that it did so because it considered softer means more effective in combatting, for example, stereotypes. The idea that policies, not laws, are most appropriate in shifting cultural beliefs, resonates with the idea that the work policy does is to 'classify and organise people in new ways' (Shore & Wright, 2011: 3).

Feminists have criticised the EU's use of soft law policy to address gendered harms as evidence of its failure to engage seriously with the issues (Walby, 2004). Lack of coherent and comprehensive policies on matters may, in part be explained by the EU's complex institutional organisation. The EU is polycentric and its bodies establish committees that, in turn, do not interact with each other or harmonise the various policies across institutions (Peterson, 2009). Yet, it is within these committees that important ideational shifts occur and often long before these positions surface on the EU political agenda (Peterson, 2009). Thus, the threshold for agreeing on harmonisation of social norms is lower than agreeing on enforcing a particular legal norm across the Union.

In some instances, the EU drives the policymaking agenda at the Member State level. At other times, policies from one or several Member States are transposed to the EU level. Mazey (1998) describes this as the difference between the nationalisation of Europe or a European agenda, and a Europeanisation of national agendas. She finds that gender equality is a good example of the latter relationship because the EU is key in establishing and transforming national gender equality agendas. This is not to say that gender equality policies and their momentum have originated with the EU. Many of these policies were a long time in the making and have gone through several iterations. They were the products of coordinated activism by second-wave feminism as a national and transnational social movement which, in the 1970s, comprised an 'advocacy coalition' in Europe (Sabatier, 1988 in Mazey, 1998: 132). We return to the role and impact of feminist advocacy below.

It is also important to recognise that the EU is a multilevel polity (Kantola, 2010). This means that the EU and its Member States are not governed in a direct sense by government in the traditional sense, but rather in the interactions between governing bodies ranging from local to supranational levels. Many EU level policies, therefore, do not only give Member States direct instructions, but also they give encouragement to governance bodies to act at other levels. In Foucault's terms, the EU appears as a dispersed governmentality that regulates and disciplines Member States and their citizens, not by force but via normative alignment. Changes over time in areas that the EU defines as within its interest transforms the nature of this alignment, and what is involved in establishing national alignment with the EU. This complex dynamic makes it particularly interesting to us as scholars of contemporary power. This means that in the context of the book, we are not concerned with discerning at *what* scale contemporary sovereignty is forged and executed through laws and policy on gender and sexuality, but rather with understanding *how* power is forged and executed via gender and sexuality discourse and practice in the form of policy.

Understanding what drives European policy development around gender and sexuality, how it impacts upon domestic developments within Member States and how it influences the relationship between the EU and its Member States is a complicated task. There is a large amount of literature that deals with this under the umbrella of European integration, which looks at the willingness of nation states to align with the EU, and the consequences thereof (Saurugger, 2014; Wiener & Diez, 2009). Integration theory as a framework has retreated from trying to explain integration and has moved towards seeing the EU as a construct to be unpacked (Diez & Wiener, 2009). Elsewhere, theoretical contributions from the field of International Relations have advanced our understanding of the EU's decision-making process (Saurugger, 2014). Researchers in this field apply different theoretical frameworks to study the relationship between different scales of governance and interests in the EU. We share these researchers' interest in how the EU governs and how EU governance is multi-scalar. We take inspiration from the growing interest in network forms of governance that:

> [R]eflects how policies to regulate modern societies, cultures, and economies are all increasingly products of mutuality and interdependence, as opposed to hierarchy and independence. Linkages between organisations, rather than organisations themselves, have become the central analytical focus for many social scientists. (Peterson, 2009: 105)

Engaging with this literature it becomes possible to identify three key assumptions that inform the study of policy networks, namely that: (1) governance, in its modern form, is non-hierarchical (both between levels and across domains, i.e., public actors are not prioritised); (2) there is great diversity across sectors and players in terms of one sector being strong and another weak, but this does not really represent what is going on in a policy network, and (3) there are a range of actors and institutions involved in producing governance, and while formal bodies are the ones who are held accountable for outcomes, it is not 'government' per se that governs (Peterson, 2009: 107). Öhlén and Silander (2020) find that how the EU is driven by a multilevel logic indicates that it is insufficient for us to look only at what happens in the Commission or indeed in Brussels. There is interaction on a range of issues between the global and local levels, and the relationship between the EU and national levels is particularly important to consider. Furthermore, Silander and Öhlén (2020) portray this relationship as 'a fusion or amalgam between the two levels of governance' (2020: 26). Again, this framing draws upon diverse and multi-scalar influences and competencies (e.g., global and local competencies and agendas, not least through how the EU and national level consult and reach agreements with actors on other levels) (ibid.: 27). Likening the EU's governance to a network or interacting layers that 'fuse' can be fruitful in terms of understanding its institutional logics and dynamics. A governance perspective appears particularly fruitful in interrogating how the EU forges gender and sexuality politics in the service of issues of high political importance. As we will discuss in the chapters that follow, within these policy areas it is evident that the interaction between organisations at the EU and national levels is disruptive to the EU governance agenda because disparate goals coexist and jockey for dominance at all levels. The EU's decision-making process fuse with decision-making processes in Member States, and the possibility for this to be coherent and fruitful differs across the Union. Differences in legal and policy-making cultures among Member States have increased normative friction in many key areas. This situation returns us to the nub of our argument relative to the dissonance and convergence between the EU and Member States acceptance of or resistance to its attempts to expand its normative powers through increased harmonisation.

Our discussion, thus far, has focussed on the EU level. Given that civil society actors are key to agenda-setting in our two areas of policy interest, namely prostitution and rape, in the following section, we examine their roles in more detail.

The Role of Civil Society Actors

Critics argue that there is a democratic deficit in the EU policy sphere in terms of its decision-making process and in terms of citizens' participation in that process (Armstrong, 2002). Legitimacy of European level governance relies on it being attached to an idea that Europe has a distinct European identity (della Porta & Caiani, 2009). Reflecting changes in the international community around civil society participation and, not least, through shifts in EU policy following from the Treaty of Maastricht and its implementation of 'social dialogue' (della Porta & Caiani, 2009), the EU has integrated various stakeholder groups in its policymaking fora. This openness to civil society participation has created opportunities for feminist actors to be active in agenda-setting and for pushing certain political programmes. Generally, feminism as a social movement has been good at influencing supranational actors' agendas (Houge et al., 2015), and its investment in making this impact must be seen in light of the criticism that representative democracy is poor at maintaining the interests of women or LGBTQI people (Chironi, 2020). In the case of the EU, its preference for the community decision-making process means that feminists can make headway in Brussels on issues that prove intractable domestically (Kantola, 2010). This must not be interpreted to mean that feminist civil society actors represent nation state grassroots organisations, as the EU has invested considerably in building and funding these actors (Mazey, 1998). This alternative political platform is often quite effective in putting pressure on national policymakers to act and address areas that otherwise they might not wish to countenance. Feminist organisations and groups at the EU level have been effective in instrumentalising this format for the advancement of their agendas in several areas. Importantly, their involvement occurs not only by aiding the development and adoption of EU Directives, but also via writing Reports that feed into non-binding Resolutions. Zippel (2004) argues that we should understand this as a situation were civil society actors are not just getting involved in a policy exchange between European and national level policymakers, but also that their involvement contributes to the decision-making processes in areas that traditionally have been considered outside the competencies of the EU. In cases such as these, the EU starts developing its involvement in any given area through soft law policies (Zippel, 2004). This observation brings us to the notion of the EU velvet triangle and the role it plays in this process.

Several kinds of civil society actors engage in meaning-making in the area of sexual politics on the national and EU levels, ranging from small national organisations working to draw attention to an aspect of contemporary gender relations to large transnational coalitions that engage on a broad range of topics (Roseneil et al., 2012). As we discussed above, Woodward (2004) coined the term the velvet triangle to describe interactions between policymakers and politicians, feminist academics and experts and the women's movement in EU policymaking. In ways that reflect the power imbalances and the hierarchy of womanhood endemic in such organisations, the velvet triangle does not represent women of colour and those who experience socio-economic disadvantage well (Elman, 2001). One should, therefore, not assume that the meaning of the category of 'women' in the velvet triangle is a unitary or unifying category that can create and deliver women-friendly policies on all areas of women's lives (FitzGerald & Freedman, 2021). It is a fact that women have different and even conflicting interests. For example, in EU institutions some feminist civil society actors gain a more prominent position than others. This is, in part, because they are willing to make trade-offs on substantive issues in order to advance their agenda. They do this by aligning themselves with the EU in ways that advance the EU's policy agenda in some area, or because they acquire certain political skills or capital through their involvement in collaborations between state and non-state actors at the national level. Sweden is a good case to highlight. It has a strong tradition of bureaucrats and politicians engaging in institutionalised exchange with civil society actors (Panke, 2010). Consequently, its engagement with the EU is characterised by a high level of activity and an active engagement in norm advocacy (Björkdahl, 2008).

The trouble with this is that feminist engagement with EU gender policy creation has entwined with governmentality and biopolitics. We argue this because it is often the case that feminist intervention in EU policy making has become a *moving target* around the *meaning* of gender and equality. Therefore, feminist politics in this area has become separated from its origins in transformative practice. When this happens, it becomes possible for those in power to instrumentalise gender in support of other issues, such as market forces. As Roseneil et al. (2012) observe, in circumstances such as these, it becomes difficult to know where the women's movement ends and the EU and market forces begin. Of course, we could also interpret this situation as a sign of the women's movement success in placing gender on supranational agendas, including the EU (Houge et al., 2015). One could argue that in order to integrate a gender perspective most efficiently, then the EU needs feminists to speak with one voice. As Cullen states, however, when summing up the literature, 'For the women's movement, evidence suggests that feminists mobilising close to institutional contexts can, over time, be incorporated into state bodies that are hollowed out or marginalised from centres of power and resources' (2015: 411). Framed thus, as the velvet triangle hollows out the meaning of gender equality, it becomes a *sitting duck* or a proxy in wider EU politics that EU policy makers can instrumentalise in the service of issues of higher political importance. This is something that critics have accused the European Women's Lobby (EWL) of doing strategically at the centres of EU power, particularly in the EP (Zippel, 2004).

We are interested in policymaking in the EU, including the networked ways in which it operates. National and regional civil society actors belong in this frame, and among them, the EWL is a particularly strong actor. The EWL is a prominent pan-European coalition with members from across the Union. Female representatives in the Commission initiated the organisation and supported its establishment in 1990 in response to the growing awareness of the need to defend women's interests at the European level. Institutional support means that 'it is a particularly important actor on a European scale' (Cullen, 2015: 411). To date, it receives about 80% of its funding from the Commission (Montoya, 2013; Strid, 2009).

The EWL prioritises VAW and considers both prostitution and rape under this umbrella term. As a norm entrepreneur, 'The EWL has been credited with maintaining a feminist presence at EU level' (Cullen, 2015: 411). Mazey (1998) noted that the EWL made it possible for the EU to establish gender equality as a common European value via the Treaty of Amsterdam (EC 1997). Although the EWL operates as a coalition, it draws on a broad range of strategies to assert its influence. It delivers expertise to EU policy processes, but also helps the EU to secure visibility and legitimacy for it policies on gender and sexuality (Mazey, 1998). In short, in the competitive EU policy sphere, gender expertise grants feminists leverage. By offering EU institutions consultancy expertise and knowledge, feminists gain access to the policy-framing sphere within the EU where they can contribute to the meaning of gender equality at the institutional level. This has given certain feminist groups, especially the EWL and the European Parliament's Committee on Women's Rights and Gender Equality (the FEMM Committee), access to power (Mazey, 1998). In this ecosystem, civil society actors operate as norm entrepreneurs on both the domestic and European levels, and as such, they contribute to establishing norm alignment across all scales of governance (Börzel & Risse, 2007). This way of organising policy development and diffusion resembles how Swedish politics, for example, operate in terms of a strong civil society presence, its engagement with the state (Montoya, 2013: 31) and with a style of governance that emphasises committees and the inclusion of external expertise (Outshoorn et al., 2012: 133).

As an institution less set in its ways than national governments, the EU offers civil society actors more opportunities to influence policies than many Member States (Zippel, 2004). The channels of influence available to civil society actors often depend on which expertise they can offer the EU (Zippel, 2004). For example, in 2007, the EWL identified combatting VAW as one of its strategic aims. A central vehicle for the EWL to achieve this has been by encouraging the EU to sign the Council of Europe Convention on Preventing and Combating Violence against Women and Domestic Violence (the Istanbul Convention).[2] We will describe this in more detail in Chapter 4, but here it suffices to note that the process by which the EU and the EWL have worked to realise this objective exemplifies both how the EWL works and to what effect.

Taken together in the context of this book this mapping exercise offers a way to talk about the EU's institutions, groups and actors who conceptualise and attempt to harmonise norms and values around European sexual politics via hard and soft law policies. Yet, as we have seen, this is a contested area. In light of the current tensions around sexual politics between the EU and some of its Member States, we use the final section of this chapter to ponder the question: Where to now for European gender and sexual policy?

---

[2] The Council of Europe is autonomous from the EU and is a European political organisation currently with 47 member states. Its foundation is the principles of the European Convention in Human Rights (ECHR).

Conclusion: Where to Now for European Gender and Sexuality Policy?

As we have outlined in this chapter, to secure and harmonise policies on gender and sexuality is a core task of the EU (Maj, 2014). This means that gender and sexuality are on the minds of European level policymakers. Mindful of the major normative and societal changes that have taken place in terms of gender and sexuality norms historically, and how these transformations have produced controversies and conflicts around culture and ideology in certain quarters, we submit that this shapes Member States' understanding of the EU and, in turn, how the EU relates to them. In this way, gender and sexuality function as *moving targets* in terms of their ability to inform meaning-making around norms and values and as *sitting ducks* apt to be taken up and redeployed strategically as proxies. This is, perhaps, unsurprising since, at its inception, the EU did not wish to influence social and legal norms on these issues across the Union.

> When the 'founding fathers' signed the 1957 Treaties of Rome, no one imagined that by 2002 the European Union would enact law addressing such a highly controversial issue as sexual harassment. Although gender inequalities persist throughout EU Member States, the development of gender equality policy in the workplace has been one of the most astonishing aspects of European integration over the past 30 years. (Zippel, 2004: 57–58)

Researchers have argued that feminist activism made this expansion possible (Elman, 1996), and that shifts in EU policies have made a considerable impact on Member States' policies to the extent that some countries have established new policy areas (Mazey, 1998). As prominent feminist civil society actors such as the EWL continue to influence the EU (Strid, 2009), it becomes necessary to ask: (1) Who do they represent? (2) Are their policy agendas inclusive? and (3) Do they constitute a feminist challenge to the EU's worst impulses? Critics have challenged what they perceive as the EWL's tendency to remove itself too far from its roots in feminist politics. To many observes organisations like the EWL have become embroiled in a symbiotic relationship with the EU that has negative effects for women (see e.g. Cullen, 2015; Lang, 2014). As we have discussed above, the velvet triangle and other feminist actors may not necessarily pursue intersectional policies (Elman, 2001).

As our analysis shows, inequalities and differences in this area exist between European nations. In 2004, ten Eastern and Central European countries acceded to the EU. Immediately, the Union became more diverse (Forest & Lombardo, 2012). Several of the new Member States from the post-communist Bloc have rejected feminism as being a valid political position. This, undoubtedly, is something that continues to permeate the region's relationships with the EU and it is something to which we will return in Chapter 5. Against this backdrop and under the banner of common European values, the EU critiques both its own members and outsiders. Europe has critiqued how non-EU countries approach LGBTQI rights, most often Russia.[3] Of course, the irony is that this eschews the fact that LGBTQI persons are in no way treated in a uniform way within the EU, where there are different levels of tolerance and equality with heterosexuals' rights and with the rights of gender-conforming people. When the EU reprimands Russia for being anti-gay, it sends a message to its Member States by re-enforcing what it considers to be European. Such a move is not unrelated to how old Member States relate to, and attempt to discipline, new Member States in Eastern (EU-25) and South Eastern Europe (EU-27).

The presence of such diversity can, perhaps, explain why the EU is more concerned with normative alignment now than previously, and why the process towards normative alignment that started decades ago is now more immediate. As we have seen, more policies supporting gender equality and LGBTQI rights do not lead automatically to their uptake at the national level. If the EU is to realise harmonisation on norms established in the EU *acquis* on gender and sexuality, then it is clear that enforcing policy alignment alone will not do the trick. As the EU takes distinct positions on how Member States should regulate gender and sexuality, some Member States resist what they perceive as EU interference on domestic matters. The Republic of Ireland (hereafter Ireland) is a good case to highlight Member States' resistance to EU values around gender and sexuality. Before 2018, when Ireland repealed the eighth amendment to the Constitution (1983), Ireland's harsh legal stance on women's human rights around access to legalised abortion brought it into direct conflict with the EU (Fletcher, 2018). And yet, as the Irish situation reveals European sexual politics are not fixed. Curiously, Ireland has

---

[3] See: http://www.lgbt-ep.eu/press-releases/meps-speak-out-against-homophobic-and-transphobic-censorship-laws-russia/.

been moving to more liberal and inclusive law and policy around gender and sexuality precisely at a time when we see the rolling back of those rights in other EU countries.

In the same vein, we need to understand that the EU and Member States may affect each other in different ways due to their different needs. This is something that also has consequences for civil society actors. In order to achieve their goals, civil society actors have to mobilise and build legitimacy on the EU's terms. As we have seen, the EU continues to prioritise arguments around gender equality, for example, based on the principles of economic rationality (Elomäki, 2015). This has implications for the topics the EU will prioritise, but it is also something that may delimit feminist civil society actors' behaviour and steer them towards issues and positions that support the EU's overall goals but that are not necessarily feminist (Elomäki, 2015: 298; Strid, 2009). Important, particularly in terms of our focus in this book, is the fact that the EU, until recently, oriented its gender equality efforts towards securing women's participation in the labour market. Consequently, it addressed sexual violence and the relationship between sexuality, gender and power only when it infringed on women's ability to participate as equal in the labour market. Repo (2015) emphasises that the EU's rationale for including gender equality was demographic. It is well-known that the EU faces challenges to its future development due to its ageing population. In the past, the EU dealt with other challenges in this area by making participation in the labour market *and* child rearing attractive to women. In this way, the EU made 'gender equality' a 'technology of power' to further its needs (Repo, 2015: 308). Repo argues that the EU was able to apply 'gender equality' to introduce measures to promote child rearing decontextualised from the welfare model, in which these measured had grown, for example those in operation in Sweden. This asserts to the flexibility of the gender argument, Repo contends:

> By applying economic language to the discussion of women's and men's personal life choices, neoliberal governmentality shifts the responsibility for governing fertility and economy to individuals themselves, who must engage in techniques of self-inspection, calculation, and self-governance. Women in particular are rendered responsible for both fertility and productivity, and hence, the well-being and prosperity of society'. (Repo, 2015: 323)

Since then, however, we witness little change and EU gender policies continue to be guided by an economic rationale (Elomäki, 2015) and the EU has refrained from developing hard law and soft law policies in areas that it considers to be 'private'. Through this policy priority it contributes to the continuation of the artificial public–private divide that feminists have fought hard to dismantle at the national level.

We find evidence of similar behaviour in the strong alignment between state and feminist organisations in Scandinavian countries, namely Norway, Sweden and Denmark. This trend established what Hernes in 1987 termed 'state feminism' or the gradual inclusion of feminist principles into state agendas. A characteristic of Swedish feminism is the way it has turned to, impacted on and been moulded by its relationship to the state. In such a context, feminist initiatives have come from both civil society and state actors. Walby points out that (2004: 14): 'there has been an increasing turn to the state and other sources of legal regulation as a focus for feminist politics'. She argues that this is due to both the emergence of opportunity structures for impact and the force of coalition building among feminist organisations. We would argue that by going mainstream and by building capacity, feminist civil society actors are turning themselves into suitable partners in policy development and implementation for governments, including those at the EU level. On the one hand, this aligns with developments in international feminism (Walby, 2004). On the other hand this resembles the kind of 'state feminism' that Swedish feminists have engaged in for many decades.

Overall, this has created opportunities for feminist civil society to shape social norms. At the same time, however, it has directed them towards particular goals and instruments which they, in turn, have used to advance their political agendas (Zippel, 2004). This means that advocates who want to influence policies have to relate to that overarching perspective of those they wish to influence, in this case by contributing to EU priorities such as securitisation, immigration control and criminal enforcement. These goals have not been beneficial to all, particularly marginalised women, migrants and a range of radicalised and sexual 'Others' (Skilbrei, 2019). In later chapters, we will return to what happens to feminism's critical potential as it contributes to external EU goals.

Drawing this chapter to a conclusion, we want to return to the point we began by noting. The EU is incorporating more and more policy areas into its competencies. This does two things at once. First, it broadens its scope and the level of its intervention capacity. Secondly and because of this, the EU adopts soft law policies to secure its objectives. It does this by enlisting a range of civil society actors as partners and norm entrepreneurs in policymaking who will assist it to harmonise the *meaning* of gender and sexuality across the Union. In this way, gender and sexuality become *moving targets*. Criticism of this approach invariably points out that the outcomes of these processes are more 'soft', non-binding measures (Peters & Pierre, 2009). This move coincides with EU expansion eastward in 2004. On this issue, Peters and Pierre (2009) ask whether 'softening us' was a prerequisite for the successful inclusion of those countries marked by other and weaker institutional traditions, that might not be compatible with the EU in its most rigid form.

Taken together, then, in the field of gender and sexuality, EU and Member States' law and policy developments are relations that emerge from the 'inside' and the 'outside', and from 'above' and 'below' and often all at the same time. This is something that makes it necessary to use a wider aperture that can help us to discern how 'epistemic communities' create meaning through 'networks of knowledge-based experts' (Haas, 1992: 2). It points to how these networks are established across divides, scales of governance and public-private divisions. Thus, in such contexts gender and sexuality become *sitting ducks* as each level of governance jockeys to establish hegemony in this area. In the remainder of the book, we will interrogate how such developments occur in practice by mapping the exchanges, responses and revisions that have taken place in the policy fields of prostitution and rape.

References

Adler-Nissen, R. (2014). *Opting out of the European Union: Diplomacy, sovereignty and European integration*. Cambridge University Press.

Ahrens, P. (2019). The birth, life, and death of policy instruments: 35 years of EU gender equality policy programmes. *West European Politics, 42*(1), 45–66.

Allwood, G. (2018). Agenda setting, agenda blocking and policy silence: Why is there no EU policy on prostitution? *Women's Studies International Forum, 69*, 126–134.

Armstrong, K. (2002). Rediscovering civil society: The European Union and the White Paper on governance. *European Law Journal, 8*(1), 102–132.

Beveridge, F. (2012). 'Going soft'? Analysing the contribution of soft and hard measures in EU gender law and policy. In E. Lombardo & M. Forest (Eds.), *The Europeanisation of gender equality policies: Gender and politics series* (pp. 28–48). Palgrave Macmillan.

Björkdahl, A. (2008). Norm advocacy: A small state strategy to influence the EU. *Journal of European Public Policy*, 15(1), 135–154. https://doi.org/10.1080/13501760701702272

Blagojevic, J. (2011). Between walls: Provincialism, human rights, sexualities and Serbian public discourses on EU integration. In R. Kulpa & J. Mizielinska (Eds.), *De-centring western sexualities: Central and Eastern European perspectives* (pp. 27–42). Ashgate.

Borchardt, K. D. (2017). *The ABC of EU law*. The European Commission. https://op.europa.eu/en/publication-detail/-/publication/5d4f8cde-de25-11e7-a506-01aa75ed71a1. Accessed 21 Sept 2021.

Börzel. T., & Risse, T. (2007). When Europe hits home: Europeanization and domestic change. *European Integration online Papers (EIoP)*, 4(15). https://doi.org/10.2139/ssrn.302768

Bulmer, S., Dolowitz, D., Humphreys, P., & Padgett, S. (2009). *Policy transfer in European Union governance: Regulating the utilities*. Routledge.

Burri, S., & Prechal, S. (2008). *EU gender equality law*. Office for Official Publications of the European Communities.

Butler, J. (2009). Sexual politics, torture, and secular time. In E. Oleksy (Ed.), *Intimate citizenships: Gender, sexuality, politics* (pp. 17–39). Routledge.

Chironi, D. (2020). A fragile shield for protecting civil rights: The European Union in the eyes of Italian feminists. *European Journal of Cultural and Political Sociology*, 7(3), 316–346.

Cullen, P. (2015). Feminist NGOs and the European Union: Contracting opportunities and strategic response. *Social Movement Studies*, 14(4), 410–426.

della Porta, D., & Caiani, M. (2009). *Social movements and Europeanization*. Oxford University Press.

Diez, T., & Wiener, T. (2009). Introducing the mosaic of integration theory. In A. Wiener & T. Diez (Eds.), *European integration theory* (2nd ed., pp. 1–22). Oxford University Press.

Dzenovska, D. (2018). *School of Europeanness: Tolerance and other lessons in political liberalism in Latvia*. Cornell University Press.

Elman, R. A. (1996). Introduction: The EU from feminist perspectives. In R. A. Elman (Ed.), *Sexual politics and the European Union: The new feminist challenge* (pp. 1–12). Berghahn Books.

Elman, R. S. (2001). Testing the limits of European citizenship: Ethnic hatred and male violence. *National Women's Studies Association Journal*, 13(3), 49–69.

Elomäki, A. (2015). The economic case for gender equality in the European Union: Selling gender equality to decision-makers and neoliberalism to women's organizations. *European Journal of Women's Studies, 22*(3), 288–302.

FitzGerald, S., & Freedman, J. (2021). Where is the justice in EU anti-trafficking policy? Feminist reflections on European Union policy-making processes. *European Journal of Women's Studies, 28*(4). https://doi.org/10.1177/13505068211029324

Fletcher, R. (2018). #RepealedThe8th: Translating travesty, global conversation, and the Irish abortion referendum. *Feminist Legal Studies, 26*, 233–259.

Forest, M., & Lombardo, E. (2012). The Europeanization of gender equality policies: A discursive-sociological approach. In E. Lombardo & M. Forest (Eds.), *The Europeanization of gender equality policies: Gender and politics series* (pp. 1–27). Palgrave Macmillan.

Foucault, M. (1977). *Discipline and punish: The birth of the prison*. Allen Lane.

Guerrina, R. (2020). Gendering the political economy of the European social model. In D. Bigo, T. Diez, E. Fanoulis, B. Rosamond, & Y. A. Stivachtis (Eds.), *The Routledge handbook of critical European studies* (pp. 95–117). Routledge.

Haas, P. (1992). Introduction: Epistemic communities and international policy coordination. *International Organisation, 49*(1), 1–35.

Hernes, H. (1987). *Welfare state and woman power: Essays in state feminism*. Norwegian University Press.

Houge, A. B., Lohne, K., & Skilbrei, M.-L. (2015). Gender and crime revisited: Criminological gender research on international and transnational crime and crime control. *Journal of Scandinavian Studies in Criminology and Crime Prevention, 16*(2), 160–174.

Jacquot, S. (2015). *Transformations in EU gender equality: From emergence to dismantling*. Springer.

Kamenou, N. (2011). Queer in Cyprus: National identity and the construction of gender and sexuality. In L. Downing & R. Gillett (Eds.), *Queer in Europe: Contemporary case studies* (pp. 25–40). Ashgate.

Kantola, J. (2010). *Gender and the European Union*. Macmillan International Higher Education.

Lang, S. (2014). Women's advocacy networks: The European Union and the velvet triangle. In I. Grewal & V. Bernal (Eds.), *Theorizing NGOs: Feminist struggles, states and neoliberalism* (pp. 266–284). Duke University Press.

Liebert, U. (2003). Gender politics in the European Union: The return of the public. *European Societies, 1*(2), 197–239.

MacRae, H., & Weiner, E. (2017). Conclusion: Common ground and new terrain. In H. MacRae & E. Weiner (Eds.), *Towards gendering institutionalism: Equality in Europe* (pp. 207–214). Rowman & Littlefield.

Maj, J. (2014). *Gender equality in the European Union: A comparative study of Poland and Germany*. Nomos.

Mazey, S. (1998). The European Union and women's rights: From the Europeanization of national agendas to the nationalization of a European agenda. *Journal of European Public Policy*, 5(1), 131–152.

Montoya, C. (2013). *From global to grassroots: The European Union, transnational advocacy, and combating violence against women*. Oxford University Press.

Öhlén, M., & Silander, D. (2020). Europeanisation, governance and policy processes. In D. Silander & M. Öhlén (Eds.), *Sweden and the European Union: An assessment of the influence of EU-membership on eleven policy areas in Sweden* (pp. 20–38). Santérus Academic Press Sweden.

Outshoorn, J., Kulawik, T., Dudová, R., & Prata, A. (2012). Remaking bodily citizenship in multicultural Europe: The struggle for autonomy and self-determination. In B. Halsaa, S. Roseneil, & S. Sümer (Eds.), *Remaking citizenship in multicultural Europe: Women's movements, gender and diversity* (pp. 118–140). Palgrave Macmillan.

Panke, D. (2010). Small states in the European Union: Structural disadvantage in the EU policy-making and counter-strategies. *Journal of European Public Policy*, 17(6), 799–817.

Peters, B., & Pierre, J. (2009). Governance approaches. In A. Wiener & T. Diez (Eds.), *European integration theory* (2nd ed., pp. 91–104). Oxford University Press.

Peterson, J. (2009). Policy networks. In A. Wiener & T. Diez (Eds.), *European integration theory* (2nd ed., pp. 105–124). Oxford University Press.

Radaelli, C. M. (2004). Europeanisation: Solution or problem? *European Integration online Papers (EIoP)*, 8(16): 1–23. http://eiop.or.at/eiop/texte/2004-016a.htm

Repo, J. (2015). *The biopolitics of gender*. Oxford University Press.

Roseneil, S., Halsaa, B., & Sümer, S. (2012). Remaking citizenship in multicultural Europe: Women's movements, gender and diversity. In B. Halsaa, S. Roseneil, & S. Sümer (Eds.), *Remaking citizenship in multicultural Europe: Women's movements, gender and diversity* (pp. 1–20). Palgrave Macmillan.

Rose, N., & Miller, P. (1992). Political power beyond the state: Problematics of government. *The British Journal of Sociology*, 43(2), 173–205.

Saurugger, S. (2014). Europeanisation in times of crisis. *Political Studies Review*, 12(2), 181–192.

Scoular, J. (2010). What's law got to do with it? How and why law matters in the regulation of sex work. *Journal of Law and Society*, 37(1), 12–39.

Shore, C., & Wright, S. (2011). Conceptualising policy: Technologies of governance and the politics of visibility. In C. Shore, S. Wrights, & D. Però (Eds.), *Policy worlds: Anthropology and the analysis of contemporary power* (pp. 1–26). Berghahn Books.

Silander, D., & Öhlén, M. (2020). Swedish politics and the EU. In D. Silander & M. Öhlén (Eds.), *Sweden and the European Union: An assessment of the influence of EU-membership on eleven policy areas in Sweden* (pp. 10–19). Santérus Academic Press Sweden.

Skilbrei, M.-L. (2019). Assessing the power of prostitution policies to shift markets, attitudes, and ideologies. *Annual Review of Criminology, 2*(1), 493–508.

Strid, S. (2009). *Gendered interests in the European Union: The European Women's Lobby and the organisation and representation of women's interests*. Örebro University.

Szulc, L. (2011). Queer in Poland. In L. Downing & R. Gillett (Eds.), *Queer in Europe: Contemporary case studies* (pp. 159–172). Ashgate.

Walby, S. (2004). The European Union and gender equality: Emergent varieties of gender regime. *Social Politics: International Studies in Gender, State & Society, 11*(1), 4–29.

Wiener, A., & Diez, T. (2009). Taking stock of integration theory. In A. Wiener & T. Diez (Eds.), *European integration theory* (2nd ed., pp. 241–252). Oxford University Press.

Woodward, A. (2004). Building velvet triangles: Gender and informal governance. In S. Piattoni & T. Christiansen (Eds.), *Informal governance and the European Union* (pp. 76–93). Edward Elgar.

Zippel, K. (2004). Transnational advocacy networks and policy cycles in the European Union: The case of sexual harassment. *Social Politics, 11*(1), 57–85.

CHAPTER 3

From Sweden to Brussels: Forging a European Agenda on Prostitution

Abstract This chapter focuses on the EU's policy response to prostitution. It begins with an historical analysis of Europe's prostitution regulatory regimes and moves to the contemporary moment. Drawing on Foucault's theories of sex, bodies, and governmentality, the chapter begins the work of building a critical feminist analysis of prostitution as an aspect of European sexual politics. Then, the chapter considers Swedish feminist politics leading up to Swedish's decision to introduce a sex purchase ban in 1999. Using Foucault's theory, the chapter interrogates the problematics driving how feminists promote the so-called 'Swedish model'. Following this, it examines how this approach has influenced feminist prostitution politics in other European jurisdictions. And finally, the chapter analyses events occurring at the EU level in this area and how these policy directions advance the EU project.

Keywords Prostitution · Regimes of governance · The French system · Sweden · Sex purchase ban · The EU

This chapter introduces how the EU considers the policy area of prostitution. In order to map European sexual politics around prostitution we divide the chapter into three sections. In Section One entitled: 'A

© The Author(s), under exclusive license to Springer Nature Switzerland AG 2022
S. FitzGerald and M.-L. Skilbrei, *Sexual Politics in Contemporary Europe*, https://doi.org/10.1007/978-3-030-91174-4_3

Genealogy of European Governance of Prostitution', we locate our analysis in its historical context in European prostitution regulatory regimes and move to the contemporary moment. In order to develop our analysis, we combine our conceptual framework around gender and sexuality as *moving targets* and *sitting ducks* in the EU policy sphere with Foucault's theories of sex, bodies and governmentality. This, we hope, provides the foundations for a critical feminist analysis of prostitution as an aspect of European sexual politics. In Section Two entitled: 'The Evolution of the 'Nordic Model'', we highlight feminist politics in the Swedish context leading up to a sex purchase ban in 1999. We approach this feminist politics in two particular ways that diverge somewhat from standard analyses. First, we invoke Foucault's theory of the body, sexuality and governmentality to map European sexual politics around prostitution. In this process we consider the problematics driving how feminists have promoted the so-called 'Swedish model'. Secondly, we interrogate how this approach resonates with and has been appropriated by existing feminist prostitution politics in other European jurisdictions. In Section Three entitled: 'Shifting Feminist Prostitution Politics at the EU Level' we consider events occurring at the EU level in this area. Our primary aim is to offer the reader a comprehensive understanding of how feminist prostitution politics contribute to European sexual politics by invoking the EU's stated aims around gender equality and, in turn, uses those aims to advance a carceral vision of justice around prostitution across the Union.

A Genealogy of European Governance of Prostitution

To be sure, there has always been great diversity in how European nations have regulated prostitution. In order to map the transformations in thinking in Europe on this issue, we begin our analysis around events from the mid-eighteenth century to the contemporary moment. This requires that we disentangle the processes by which the idiom of 'the prostitute' becomes entwined in wider systems of governance, and through which European states deploy new ways of regulating their citizens' bodies and their national territories (Rose et al., 2006).

At this point, Foucault's (2003) theorisation of governmentality and biopolitics is useful, since that work contains a good exposition of the eighteenth-century proliferation rather than repression of discourses on sex and the body. Furthermore, we find that his terminology is suitable to interrogate contemporary EU policymaking, wherein Member States and their citizens are governed through soft law measures that enable them to self-govern (Lemke, 2013). We do not find it particularly innovative to approach prostitution law and policy as rational responses to a problem to be solved, but rather we are interested in how the EU forms a particular understanding of the 'problem of prostitution' and designs policy solutions to address it. Governmentality, then, brings together ways of acting (governmental technologies) and ways of thinking (political rationalities) as key to contemporary ways of ruling (Rose & Miller, 1992: 175).

Genealogy became Foucault's (1972) method of analysing discourses, which he identified as historically variable ways of creating power relations through specifying knowledge and truth. Crucially, he used genealogy not to determine *who had power*, but rather to illuminate and problematise the *exercise of power* through 'the production of truth as specific forms of knowledge' or discourse (Foucault, 1972: 93). For Foucault, then, the individual's experience of domination is an 'effect' of power rather than proceeding 'from a specific source of power' (1977: 27). This interpretation requires that the researcher and the reader understand the importance of the question of *who* exercises power in prostitution law and policy, for example, alongside *how* they deploy it.

Foucault rejected the notion of 'a theory of power' in favour of what he termed his 'analytic of power', which was based on his rejection of the 'repressive hypothesis' (1980: 15). This hypothesis suggested that, from the mid-eighteenth century onwards, western discourses repressed all discussions of sex. By contrast, Foucault argued that during this period a proliferation of discourses of sex and the body occurred. His detailed analysis of the influence of the state and the legal and medical professions on the deployment of multiple techniques of power illustrated how western ideology inserted 'sex into discourse' (Foucault, 1980: 16).

Important within this paradigm was how, from that time onwards, the biopolitics of sex in the West changed. European governments sought new ways to regulate the conduct of inhabitants of a territory. They did this not through intense discipline but through 'micro powers' that enabled them to 'conduct people's conduct' but by 'ruling from a distance' (Foucault, 2003: 192). Foucault referred to this calculative form of discipline as 'governmentality', and he defined the regulation of the population as 'biopolitics' (2003: 192). He argued that this occurred in order to 'locate new forms of power and to influence and control the ways it operated to influence the individual's behaviour' (Foucault, 1980: 16). This phenomenon made all matters pertaining to sex and the body a matter of 'public concern' and vital to managing 'certain populations' (Foucault, 1980: 71).

As European states attempted to expand forms of discipline to broader scales such as territories, and concentrated on multiple techniques of governmentality that focused on the individual's conduct of conduct, the dominant European classes began to use 'sexuality' as 'a strategy that produced … a docile body that may be subjected, used, transformed and improved' (Foucault, 1977: 28). By the turn of the nineteenth century, the European middle classes became particularly preoccupied with 'creating a class body identifiable through health, hygiene and descent' (Foucault, 1989: 124). Sex became part of a wider racialised and gendered lexicon—a *moving target*—that enabled them to articulate a class-based discourse around the meaning of morality. This entered the political discourse and governments used it as an index of the nation's strength, revealing national political potency and biological vigour. Scoular observes that this shift in thinking around sex, the body and populations is key to the creation of the modern 'prostitute subject' (2015: 33).

The nineteenth-century French system of medical policing of prostitution is an archetype of Foucault's theories of the intersection of sex, bodies, governmentality and biopolitics. In 1802, in response to an increase in the numbers of women and men infected by venereal diseases in France, the French government issued a Decree that mandated that all prostitutes submit to mandatory health inspections (Corbin, 1990). Just two years later, Napoleon Bonaparte ordered the Prefect of the Paris Police to legalise and regulate brothels. As an expression of governmentality, the government rolled out this policy nationwide, using the brigade des moeur (the vice squad) to control sex workers and to manage brothels. This system prohibited soliciting and sex workers had to register at their local prefecture in order to work in a brothel. A consequential effect of regulation on this scale was that it subjected sex workers to widespread and arbitrary extra-judicial and custodial police control and arrest for minor offences. Moreover, the gendered dimensions of this model were stark because only women had to submit twice-weekly to mandatory health checks. If the authorities suspected that a sex worker was carrying syphilis, then they could hospitalise her indefinitely (Walkowitz, 1980).

Eventually, the regulationist model for medical policing of prostitution spread to other European cities (e.g., Zurich, Madrid and Berlin) (Bristow, 1982). As Europe grappled with unprecedented social change due to the industrial revolution, especially in urban areas, social upheaval blurred class boundaries (Gilman, 1985). This fed the middle classes' anxieties about the need to surveil class boundaries in order to protect the body politic from the 'degenerate', 'criminal' and 'dangerous' working classes (McClintock, 1995: 46). Middle-class paranoia around the working classes as vectors of disease and contagion paved the way for what Gilman described as the 'institutionalisation of fear around degeneracy' that touched and transformed all aspects of nineteenth-century European social life (1985: vix).

One place where such fears were iterated was around the need to control sexuality and, in particular, the female prostitute (Waites, 2005). We can glimpse the pervasive mechanisms at work in that discursive field by turning our attention towards how prostitution became a *sitting duck* or a proxy in the wider politics around the UK government's decision in the 1860s to introduce a series of Contagious Diseases Acts (CDAs).[1] While the government claimed that it introduced the legislation to protect women from the harm of prostitution, McClintock has argued that Parliament designed the laws 'less to abolish prostitution than to place the control of sex work in the hands of the male state' (1995: 288). Read at this more granular level, the Acts serve less to give power to the state and more to create a dispersed governmentality. Therefore, in their scope and reach, the Acts' purpose was not to localise power in any one institution or governing body, but rather they created a dispersed governmentality through biopolitics that targeted one population. This operated through medical interventions, law and policing in ways that brought working class women's bodies under direct governmental control (Scoular, 2015).

The politics of controlling certain women's bodies and sexuality were not just the purview of middle-class men. By the late nineteenth century, a coalition of middle-class female campaigners united in their opposition to the Acts. They established the Ladies National Association (LNA) in 1869 to challenge the Acts, which they perceived as unconstitutional, discriminatory and 'instrumental rape' of women by doctors through forced medical examinations (Scoular, 2015: 46). Core to their politics was the

---

[1] Influenced by the continental systems, the UK Parliament introduced legislation to police prostitution via a series of Contagious Diseases Acts in 1864, 1866, and 1869.

belief in the wrongs of prostitution. Later, in 1874, Josephine Butler founded the International Abolitionist Federation (IAF), which sought to eradicate prostitution, its third party organisation and its implicit support of the patriarchal sexual double standard. Eventually, and due to widespread public outcry, abolitionists' efforts resulted in a Parliamentary motion that led to the government's decision to repeal the Acts in 1886. Despite this, biopower continued to manifest itself in other arenas around prostitution and working class women, such as the social purity movement and Magdalene laundries for 'fallen' women and girls (Walkowitz, 1980). In order to promote the cause, the government introduced the Criminal Law Amendment Act (1885) which aimed to protect young women's sexual innocence by restricting their sexual autonomy and prohibiting men from engaging in homosexual sexual relations. In fact, this piece of legislation formed the legal basis for the regulation (and persecution) of male homosexuals in Britain until 1967 (Scoular, 2015).

It would be wrong, however, to assume that these feminist campaigners shared a similar understanding of or aims on this issue (Laite, 2012). In ways that mirror contemporary feminist prostitution politics at the EU level, prostitution was a *moving target* around the meaning of the harm of prostitution among feminists and in disputes around how to address it (Walkowitz, 1980). In short, feminist campaigners understood prostitution from their middle class position in social relations. Consequently, it became a *sitting duck* or a proxy when they lobbied the government to repeal the Acts. This meant that they did not seek recognition for working class and sex-working women's experiences of marginalisation, inequality and poverty. Instead, they asked men to protect 'Other' women from men and, in the process, advanced their political agendas as middle class women (Scoular, 2015).

Due to the repeal movement's success, feminists joined forces with other middle class Christian reformers in the social purity movement across Europe. In this way, they broadened the aperture of their regulatory 'gaze' and expanded their political reach geographically. Now, these same abolitionists focused on prostitution at the international level by highlighting the scourge of so-called 'white slavery' or the moral panic around the transportation of women and girls overseas for mass prostitution, which they argued served the needs of colonial troops.

It was this step change in feminist prostitution politics that piced European governments' and the wider international community's concern with human trafficking. Consequently, in 1902, international moral outrage about the white slave trade led the French government to convene the first International Conference on the White Slave Trade in Paris (Pliley, 2010). The conference led to the draft of the first International Agreement for the Suppression of the White Slave Trade. This, in turn, provided the first definition of what would later become the established definition of trafficking in persons within the Protocol to Prevent, Suppress and Punish Trafficking in Persons especially Women and Children, supplementing the United Nations Convention against Transnational Organised Crime (the Palermo Protocol) (2000). States signed and ratified the draft instrument in 1904 (Allain, 2017). In 1910, at the Second International Convention for the Suppression of the White Slave Traffic, delegates broadened the scope of the crime to include recruitment for prostitution within national borders (Lammasniemi, 2020).

After the first world war, the international community resumed their collaboration on regulating prostitution and the attendant issue of sex trafficking. Eventually, the League of Nations assumed responsibility for this work, leading to the 1921 International Convention for the Suppression of the Traffic in Women and Children.[2] Thus for a brief period of time, the abolitionist view gained traction in European and international political circles, leading to the appointment of key women to committee positions in the League of Nations deliberations (Plinley, 2010). And yet, in the intervening period between the two world wars, abolitionists' authority began to wane. By the 1930s, the 'problem' of domestic prostitution retreated or disappeared altogether as a policy issue in Europe. Again, in ways that mirrored nineteenth-century sexual politics around prostitution, many European jurisdictions resumed their earlier approach to prostitution. For example, France introduced the 'Marthe Richard law' (1946).[3] This law had at least two legal consequences: first, it increased the State's control of prostitution; and secondly, it prohibited in places other than brothels, most noticeably in the streets. Eventually, France closed its state run brothels in 1960 (Mathieu, 2004).

During this period, European prostitution politics oscillated between disciplinary power (criminal law) and governmentality (tolerance as long as women self-regulated and it served other political agendas). Although

---

[2] Full text available at: https://treaties.un.org/doc/Publication/UNTS/LON/Volume%209/v9.pdf. Accessed 19 August 2020.

[3] *Loi n°46–685 dite Marthe Richard du 13 avril 1946* is better known as the Marthe Richard law from the name of this Member of Parliament.

European countries adopted the French system, they did not always enforce it as long as prostitutes' behaviour fell within the parameters of prescribed behaviours (e.g. they submitted to health checks, etc.). During the twentieth century, European nations adopted a mix of criminal law provisions, police by-laws and poverty laws to manage prostitution. Thus, instead of producing a unified policy on prostitution, this period was marked by an increase in biopolitical measures designed to target prostitution as public nuisance. In short, prostitution became a *sitting duck*.

Perhaps indicative of the dynamic nature of sexual politics surrounding prostitution, the Convention for the Suppression of the Traffic in Persons and of the Exploitation of the Prostitution of Others (1949), reflected international ambivalence around abolitionism because very few countries signed the Convention.[4] The Convention betrays some of the contestation and ambiguity between jurisdictions surrounding how law responds to prostitution. For example, it outlaws the exploitation of the prostitution of others, but it also considers prostitution as a private matter, which should not involve the registration and medical monitoring of individuals. These tensions notwithstanding, the Convention served as a template for much domestic legislation based on the deregulation of prostitution per se and the criminalisation of third party brokerage in Europe until the late twentieth century.

So far in this chapter we have been mapping the history of European sexual politics around prostitution up to the mid-twentieth century. We have seen how prostitution became a *moving target* around the meaning of prostitution and a *sitting duck* in the advancement of particular political agendas. In the following section, we take up this story of European sexual politics around prostitution in the 1980s. We will continue to unpack the discourses, systems of governmentality and biopower in contemporary policymaking at the EU and the Member State levels. We will commence our analysis in the next section by concentrating first on the rise of the radical feminist-inspired Nordic model that criminalises sex purchase and of which Sweden is a good example. In particular, we want to outline how neo-abolitionism becomes hegemonic by promoting an understanding of prostitution as a problem of gender inequality and

---

[4] Available at: https://ec.europa.eu/anti-trafficking/sites/antitrafficking/files/un_convention_for_the_suppression_of_the_traffic_in_persons_1949_en_1.pdf. Accessed 19 August 2020.

VAW. We stress that this is not a digression into Swedish sexual politics around prostitution. Instead, by engaging with how Swedish feminists have lobbied to introduce a sex purchase ban 'at home', we argue that this can illuminate the trajectory of prostitution politics 'out there' and particularly across the EU.

The Evolution of the 'Nordic Model'

In 1999, the Act Prohibiting the Purchase of Sexual Services came into force in Sweden. What is curious about Sweden's decision to introduce this legislation is that it occurrs in circumstances where prostitution levels are low relative to other European nations (Askola, 2007). From outside that context, one could be forgiven for thinking that Sweden introduces this law in response to a new or changing set of domestic social circumstances. This, however, is not the case. The issue was neither that prostitution was proliferating nor that the circumstances in which it operated were changing or that society viewed it as a pressing problem. But rather, in the hands of certain feminists actors, prostitution became a *moving target*, which they used strategically to change the social meaning of gender equality relative to male sexual desire and individual misfortune (Erikson, 2019).

There is an interesting tension in this framing exercise that we need to address. In the 1960s and 1970s, Sweden was associated with liberal sexual norms (Arnberg & Marklund, 2016; see also Kulick, 2005). It decriminalised certain sexual acts that, in other jurisdictions at the time, were deemed both immoral and illegal, such as pornography. This prompts questions about why, in a society based on increased liberalisation of social mores around sexuality, did Swedish feminists make the relatively marginal political issue of prostitution 'a matter of public concern' (Foucault, 1980: 71). There are several possible answers to this question. One is that in certain quarters of Swedish society since the 1990s, fears about changes to Swedish culture and values due to its accession to the EU would alter Sweden for the worse, and if nothing was done, then 'Brothel Europe' would corrupt Sweden (Kulick, 2003: 231). Another answer to this questions is that Sweden's liberalisation of sexuality resulted in a social backlash as feminists and children's advocates feared that such liberalisation normalised the sexual abuse of minors (Skilbrei & Holmström, 2013). Therefore, while prostitution was indeed a marginal issue, feminists were able to harness it to other issues of social concern. In this way, they brought it in from the margins and submitted it to public political debate. This strategy is something that we will return to again below when we discuss Swedish feminists' political activities in the EU.

The above discussion suggested that Sweden's journey towards the criminalisation of sex purchase began in the 1970s with the establishment of social work programmes directed at sex workers, as well as social science research and social work reports that addressed the link between prostitution and social problems. In this way, prostitution became a *moving target*. Sweden began to re-define the meaning of prostitution as less about individual hardship and more as a consequence of structural inequalities that forced some individuals to engage in commercial sex (Skilbrei & Holmström, 2013). Once this understanding of the meaning of prostitution as a social and not a personal problem took hold in the political imaginary, then the first shoots of what would later become known internationally as the 'Swedish model' took hold and began to flourish (Svanström, 2004). And yet, it would be a mistake to assume that criminalisation was a foregone conclusion at this stage in the political process. Rather, it would be more accurate to view events as a gradual process, through which feminists make the meaning of prostitution a contested issue and, in the process, it became a *sitting duck* that could be instrumentalised to introduce Swedish society to new ideas around social and normative values on gender and sexuality and to convince it that legislative change was necessary.

It is useful to pause here and consider the wider sexual politics that support legislative change in Sweden. Holmström and Skilbrei (2017) have noted that discourses around the relationship between the meaning of gender and power were core to Sweden's political debates around commercial sex. Beginning in the 1970s, various civil society groups including feminist grassroots organisations challenged what they perceived as Sweden's acceptance of prostitution. They argued that this was incompatible with the meaning of Swedish values, and in this way, they inserted discourses of prostitution, gender and sexuality into the fabric of a particular kind of Swedish identity politics (Yttergren & Westerstrand, 2016).

Furthermore, they questioned whether extant legislation was fit for its purpose, and they called for new legislation that would enforce client criminalisation (Skilbrei & Holmström, 2013). At this time, however, they lacked Parliamentary support for this policy direction. By contrast, a small but vocal group supported the status quo. They questioned the emerging discursive frame and asked whether prostitution constituted a problem per se. Instead, they focused on the need for continued social interventions to address commercial sex and a range of other social problems that perpetuated inequality. Consequently, they took a different view about the locus of the problem and called for the deregulation of prostitution (Erikson, 2019). Developing this point requires that we continue to explore how Swedish feminists' constitution of the meaning of problem of prostitution and the tactics they offered to solve it became hegemonic through their continued iteration of two interconnected discourses, namely: (i) prostitution is a societal problem and (ii) prostitution is a gendered problem. Let us consider these framing devices in turn.

First, during the 1980s and after much political deliberation, disparate voices agreed on the meaning of prostitution. Put simply: it constituted a social problem that required mitigating state action (Erikson, 2019). As dominant feminist voices began to converge and together moved into political space to manage their public message, they argued that Sweden needed to amend its penal code on prostitution. The upshot of what seemed like consensus is that this limited the possibilities for non-aligned groups and sex workers to challenge the dominant view. Secondly, and as dominant feminists filled political space physically and discursively with their rhetoric, they advanced their position by introducing another discourse into the debate (Erikson, 2017). Influenced by radical feminist thinking that understood prostitution as a gender equality issue rooted in patriarchy and unequal social structures that disadvantaged women (MacKinnon, 1987), feminists identified the male client as the locus of inequality in prostitution. In this frame, the male client was both the vehicle for harm but also someone who was harmed by prostitution. It is important to note, however, at this time feminist debates were biased towards criminalising both parties or neither. It is at this juncture that we can identify the emergence of yet another discourse in this political space. Swedish feminists insisted that the seller of sex (read female) needed protection and the buyer (read male) had to be punished (Svanström, 2004).

Ultimately, it was the latter configuration of discourses that gave this feminist frame hegemony in Sweden. As feminists continued to assert themselves politically, they refined their discursive frame. Eventually, they achieved their ambition when the Swedish government introduced legislation to criminalise sex purchase as part of the Women's Peace Bill (Government of Sweden, 1998). Lawmakers stated that in introducing the law their aim was to reduce prostitution in the short term through stricter policing, and to change the public's attitudes towards sex purchasing in the long term. Interestingly, while human trafficking did not figure prominently in feminist debate leading up to legislative change in Sweden, the government stated that it hoped the new laws would also help it to tackle sex trafficking (Holmström & Skilbrei, 2017). Although lawmakers framed the Act in gender-neutral terms, 'the intervention model is explicitly gendered in that its aims to target men's actions and attitudes' (Holmström & Skilbrei, 2017: 83).

While several researchers have evaluated the Act (for discussion, see Danna, 2012; Dodillet & Östergren, 2011; Holmström & Skilbrei, 2017; Levy & Jakobsson, 2014; Vuolajärvi, 2019), to date no longitudinal study has been conducted of Sweden's reformed prostitution laws (Scoular & FitzGerald, 2021). The Act provoked a debate that illustrated the ambivalence of the evidence supporting the law's positive effects. For example, a study conducted by a government appointed committee indicated that prosecution levels were low (Government of Sweden, 2010). Even though the law criminalised sex purchase irrespective of its location, empirical work found that enforcement was arbitrary, with the main focus being on the visible spaces of street prostitution in the three largest Swedish cities (Olsson, 2021). This reality prompts researchers to conclude that criminalisation addresses prostitution's public aspects, but it ignores its private dimensions by displacing rather than abolishing the sex market (Hubbard et al., 2008).

While the Swedish model is more readily equated with a particular piece of Swedish legislation—the Sex Purchase Act—it is also associated with decriminalisation of the sale of sex and social work. While the new legislation did not include the decriminalisation of the sale of sex, neo-abolitionists in other jurisdictions have interpreted it thus. The point is that references to the Swedish model have served as both an elastic discourse and tactic for attempts to criminalise sex purchase in other jurisdictions; in short, it is a *moving target* in domestic political and legal debates (FitzGerald & McGarry, 2016). As neo-abolitionists in other jurisdictions hail it as the panacea to the problem of prostitution, their attempts to translate the approach into their contexts invariably fall short of their goals (Carline & Scoular, 2017; Ward & Wylie, 2014). Research from the Nordic region points to the damage that can occur when law-

and policy-makers ignore the contexts in which commercial sex occurs, while simultaneously overlooking the important question of how jurisdictions with different cultural, socio-economic and legislative traditions and capacities will implement the ban and what consequences this will have for those who are subject to the law. Skilbrei (2019) concludes that it is counterproductive to attempt to transpose the Swedish model elsewhere without due consideration to these factors.

This brings us to another important issue in Sweden's sexual politics that is relevant in other contexts and central to our purpose in this book. While the White Papers issued in the process leading up to Sweden's legislative change around prostitution included interviews with sex workers, sex workers were not part of the consultation process. This returns us to Foucault's (1977) analytics of power around sexuality. The government claimed that it introduced the Sex Purchase Act to ensure a better and more gender equal society, and that this made the Act equally relevant to all women and men in Sweden. Östergren (2018) noted, however, that as the Swedish campaign around legislative change gained momentum, the public sphere became an undemocratic space where sex workers' and their supporters' views became irrelevant as the feminist steamroller moved closer to its ultimate goal. In terms that resonate with Foucault's analytics of power, this reveals something of the power relationships in feminist prostitution politics as a form of governmentality and biopower. It speaks to *who* exercises power alongside *how* they do it. It reveals how certain feminist have become implicated in biopolitics that are organised around a specific population—sex-working women—and their supposed vulnerability to harm become proxies in the advancement of a particular vision of gender equality.

Importantly, particularly in terms of this book's focus, this is a strategy that oscillates between prostitution being both a *moving target* and a *sitting duck*. This dynamic has taken root in other parts of the EU. Therefore in the following section. we want to interrogate the diffusion of this particular and geo-specific form of carceral feminism (Bernstein, 2007) across the Union in the following section. Therefore, we widen our aperture again to consider how discourses around the need to criminalise sex purchase in support of gender equality have diffused beyond Sweden's feminist political circles, giving neo-abolitionists working within EU institutions, such as the European Parliament (hereafter the EP), far-reaching clout.

Shifting Feminist Prostitution Politics at the EU Level

Two major schools of thought shape contemporary feminist thinking on prostitution at the EU level. As we saw in the Swedish context above, the first perspective took inspiration from radical feminist neo-abolitionism that argued that prostitution reflected the continued patriarchal structure of society that shaped all women's lives and gender relations (Jeffreys, 2008). Female prostitutes are the quintessential victims of oppression by males who predominantly manage, organise and profit from prostitution (Barry, 1995). Thus, for them, prostitution's existence contravenes feminist commitments to gender equality, as it is a crime of violence against *all* women. Such discourse informs new legislation and policy in EU jurisdictions like the Republic of Ireland (FitzGerald & McGarry, 2016) and France (Le Bail et al., 2019).

The second perspective is a sex worker human rights perspective that argues that many women and men work voluntarily as domestic and transborder sex workers (Anderson & Andrijasevic, 2008). Accordingly, sex workers should have the same rights and protections as other workers, including freedom from fear, exploitation and violence (Kempadoo, 2003). Thus, while advocates acknowledge that there are abuses associated with sex work, they argue that commercial sex need not be inherently exploitative. Furthermore, they argue that it is those attempts to abolish prostitution, and the attitudes that underpin such attempts, which perpetuate abusive climates for sex workers that must be changed (Saunders, 2005). Such thinking frames law and policy measures in jurisdictions like New Zealand, which has removed prostitution from its penal code and addresses it through health, labour and taxation law as well as wider social policies (Abel & Fitzgerald, 2010).

As we have discussed previously, the EU has declined thus far to take a definitive stance on prostitution per se, arguing that it is outside its competencies and, therefore, a matter for domestic legal regimes to address. As a jurisdiction, however, the EU is free to establish a normative European position via other means. An examination of EU's soft law policy documents is instructive because it elucidates how, over time, the EU and, in particular, the EP, has changed its attitude to prostitution.

After decades on the margins of European feminist politics, prostitution re-emerged on the European policy agenda in 1986. Specifically, this occurred when feminists working in the EP's Committee on Women's

Rights and Gender Equality (the FEMM Committee) drafted a Resolution on VAW, which introduced the need to strengthen laws across the EU to protect sex workers from sexual violence. Interestingly, when the Resolution focused on prostitution, it reflected little of the neo-abolitionist rhetoric around criminalisation of clients' behaviour to protect sex workers from harm that would come to dominate future EP policy statements on prostitution. Instead, the Resolution promoted decriminalising the profession and institutionalising recognition of sex workers' citizenship rights before the law (European Parliament, 1986).

By 1997, however, we can detect a step change in the rhetoric of the FEMM Committee in this area. Why did this occur? Commentators observe that this change owes much to Sweden's accession to the EU (Jacquot, 2015; Kantola, 2010). When Sweden joined the EU in 1995 its political representatives became involved in developing policies in areas to do with gender and sexuality. Therefore, as Swedish feminists assumed their positions in EU institutions such as the EP, they brought with them their understanding of prostitution as a gender equality problem that is rooted in VAW (Mazur, 2001). In 1997, and perhaps as a reflection of the speed at which their ideas around prostitution gained traction at the EU level, Marianne Eriksson—the Swedish representative in the EP—became the FEMM Committee rapporteur. Subsequently, Eriksson drafted the report that would inform the framing of prostitution in the subsequent Parliament *Resolution on the need to establish an EU-wide campaign for zero tolerance of violence against women* (1997).[5]

Over the course of the next two decades, it is possible to trace how prostitution becomes a *moving target* in the EP. For example and in terms that seem to take inspiration from Sweden, the FEMM Committee begins I to frame the meaning of prostitution as a gender equality issue. Furthermore, the FEMM Committee's policy recommendations seem to retrieve and redeploy key Swedish framing devices as they define prostitution as a 'social problem' that perpetuates 'gender-based violence' in which women are reduced to 'commodities' (European Parliament, 1997). It is notable that by 1997 the EP no longer prioritises sex workers' rights and personhood before the law; but rather, in ways that mirror their Swedish feminists' problem representation of prostitution, all Parliamentary Reports and Resolutions direct the EU's 'gaze' onto

[5] Available at: https://op.europa.eu/en/publication-detail/-/publication/894ae31d-35dc-48cc-9bdc-cf6fbd7d94ff/language-en. Accessed 20 June 2021.

male clients' behaviour as the locus on the problem. A frame that gives a flavour of this policy trajectory emerges when the FEMM Committee insists that the EU and its EU Member States adopt a harsher stance on prostitution because it represents 'a formidable barrier to efforts to overcome inequality between women and men' (European Parliament, 1997). Failure to do so, it declared, would mean that the EU was not compliant with its own stated norms and values on gender equality.

As the EU entered the new millennium, the EP's soft law policies in this area reflected the gradual entrenchment of a governmental approach to prostitution at the EU level. In this way, prostitution became a *sitting duck* of proxy used to advance other EU level policy priorities. Throughout this period, Swedish feminists retained their positions of authority within the velvet triangle described in Chapter 2, and in the EP via its FEMM Committee by drafting a series of reports (European Parliament, 2004) that led to Parliament Resolutions (2005, 2009, 2011). Taken together, these soft law policy documents assumed an increasingly carceral stance on prostitution. Nowhere is it possible to witness the degree to which feminists have succeeded in institutionalising their vision of gender equality justice as carceral justice more than in a Report (2014) (hereafter The Honeyball Report)[6] leading to EP Resolution *on sexual exploitation and sex work and its impact on gender equality* (2014).[7]

In 2013, Mary Honeyball—the then British FEMM EP rapporteur—drafted a report.[8] The report emerged at a time when the EP had expanded legislative power within the EU (Jacquot, 2015). The Honeyball Report framed prostitution as a form of VAW, and argued that the EU should legislate it as a crime of violence. In terms that resonate with Foucault's (1977) theory of sex and bodies, Honeyball works within a specific discursive frame to locate forms of power and to influence the ways, in which the EU views all sex workers as victims of sexual exploitation. The dialectic at work here involved discourses that imposed a particular meaning on sex workers as victims and not as workers (moving

---

[6] Available at: https://www.europarl.europa.eu/doceo/document/A-7-2014-0071_EN.pdf. Accessed 19 July 2021.

[7] Available at: https://www.europarl.europa.eu/doceo/document/A-7-2014-0071_EN.html. Accessed 19 July 2021.

[8] Available at: https://www.europarl.europa.eu/sides/getDoc.do?pubRef=-//EP//NONSGML+REPORT+A7-2014-0071+0+DOC+PDF+V0//EN&language=EN. Accessed 26 August 2020.

targets) in order to shape public and institutional perceptions of prostitution and garner support for criminalisation of sex purchase (sitting ducks). Indeed, the Resolution states that 'prostitution and forced prostitution are [...] both a cause and a consequence of gender inequality which it aggravates further' (European Parliament, 2014). Invoking the loaded language of the nineteenth century reformers around the white slave trade, the report states that 'prostitution and forced prostitution are forms of slavery incompatible with human dignity and fundamental rights' (ibid.). Eventually, the Report's call for the criminalisation of sex purchase reached the EP and the FEMM Committee more broadly, which in turn, supported the EWL position and approved a motion as an EP Resolution (2014). In 2014, the EP voted in favour of adopting a Resolution based on the Honeyball Report, suggesting that EU Member States decriminalise selling sex while criminalising sex purchase. In the process, in the EU imaginary prostitution and slavery became conflated (European Parliament, 2014).

While the EU has establishes gender equality as a common EU value, we argue that the feminist discursive manoeuvre that links prostitution with trafficking is a necessary step to secure EU support. The Honeyball Report had to extend the scope and reach of the negative effects of commercial sex on the body politic by relocating it in policy areas that were of concern to the EU and its Member States alike. Therefore, the EP presented the Resolution to the EU in a press release with the heading: 'Punish the client, not the prostitute',[9] wherein the EP' summarised its position as: '[The EP] stresses that prostitution violates human dignity and human rights, whether it is forced or voluntary'. By equating prostitution with exploitation and violence, and by conflating prostitution and sex trafficking, the EWL made prostitution relevant to the EU and its Member states in other policy area. In the process, this frame-setting exercise has had negative impacts on those individuals it has claimed to protect, namely sex-working women. In short, the statement makes their opinions about their bodies and their choices about their work irrelevant, as prostitution, according to the Honeyball Report, is always problematic, even when sex workers engage in it consensually. Problematizing the taken for granted character of the policy as one of gender equality, Subrahmanian notes: 'To an external observer, this policy seems at odds

---

[9] Available at: https://www.europarl.europa.eu/news/en/press-room/20140221IPR3 6644/punish-the-client-not-the-prostitute. Accessed 24 April 2021.

with developments elsewhere that increasingly recognise sex workers' agency as a mediating variable in determining policy responses to sex work and trafficking' (2009: 111).

And yet, this mediation of feminist prostitution politics and its incursion into the EU policy space as a dimension of gender equality has not been without contestation. Outshoorn (2015) argues that prostitution is an area where national agendas have affected European level policies. In the case of the Netherlands, Outshoorn argues that 'Dutch feminists have been highly instrumental in setting the issue of voluntary prostitution and sex work on the agenda of the Council of Europe and in the European Parliament and promoting the distinction between prostitution and trafficking' (2015: 78). Commenting on this situation, Mattson (2016) observes that, against a backdrop marked by divisive feminist politics around the criminalisation/decriminalisation of prostitution, a network of government and NGO actors who promote different national and grassroots interests has materialised.

At first blush, it is possible to conclude that irrespective of feminist lobbying, the majority of EU institutions remain relatively silent on prostitution. Commentators observe that the EU's structure and the lack of convergence on policies and values across Member States render agenda denial and non-intervention the norm (Euchner & Engeli, 2018). Furthermore, they point to the EU's horizontal and consensus-seeking policymaking process, which means that policymakers and other stakeholders have difficulty getting controversial issues like prostitution onto the agenda (Allwood, 2018). By contrast, other researchers argue that, in the contemporary moment, neo-abolitionism constitutes a political and ideological statement of intent that, at the EU level, has normative consequences as Member States take their lead from Brussels and introduce sex purchase bans in their respective jurisdictions (Ward & Wylie, 2017). The EU's reluctance to intervene on this issue notwithstanding, Rubio Grundell notes that the EP's decision to adopt the 2014 Resolution delineates 'a significant intervention in contemporary sex work debates' (2021: 5). It indicates that it has a preference for the Swedish model (Allwood, 2018).

Taken together, the ways in which this has occurred highlights how certain feminists working in EU institutions have assumed a role in agenda-setting through national interventions and advocacy networks to push the criminalisation of sex purchase. As Outshoorn (2018) notes, EP's stance rescales domestic prostitution policy and integrates it at the EU level. In this vein, the EWL harnessed its political agenda to core

EU policy priorities by attempting to reframe prostitution as a breach of European values pertaining to gender equality. It states that 'persistence of systems of prostitution in EU Member States is a strong indicator of the failure of Europe as a whole to engage in reaching gender equality and promoting women's rights' (Scoular, 2015: 10). Thus, the EWL describes the EU as contravening its own treaties and unable to uphold European values. Commenting on its policy agenda, the EWL stated:

> Furthermore, we argue below that the political opportunity structure of the EU became systematically more favourable in the 1990s, as a result of the adoption of the Maastricht Treaty on European Union in 1993, and the subsequent accession in 1995 of three new member states with a longstanding commitment to sexual equality. These changes explain much of the recent broadening of the EU women's rights agenda. (Pollack & Hafner-Burton, 2000: 434)

And yet, the on the ground reality is that the meaning of gender equality for European women remains contested. The problem associated with achieving consensus across the Union on controversial issues comes into sharp relief around the issue of prostitution. Consider the following examples. In 1999, when Sweden adopted legislation to criminalise sex purchase that same year, the Netherlands lifted its ban on brothels, making indoor and outdoor prostitution legal in toleration zones (*tippelzones*). Then, Germany revised its *Strafgesetzbuch* (criminal code) and its *Bürgerliches Gesetzbuch* (civil codes) in 2001, and introduced the *Prostitutiongesetz* (the Prostitution Act 2001), which came into force in 2002. This legislative reform reclassified prostitution, which the German civil law understood as *sittenwidrig* (or an offence against morality) (FitzGerald, 2020). Legislative change removed this moral frame and focused instead on sex workers' working conditions. This situation reveals that while divergent understandings and approaches to prostitution continue to exist across Europe, in recent years, we can also identify a trend whereby prostitution and its regulation have become increasingly entwined with national identity politics. In short, prostitution has become a *sitting duck* and apt to be redeployed in strategic and often problematic ways. For example, in the Republic of Ireland, debates around the need for legislative change regarding prostitution were explicit in certain stakeholders' use of national identity politics to push for a sex purchase ban. Invoking the Swedish model as the gold standard on European gender equality, delegates from the Turn off the Red Light campaign (ToRL)—an Irish neo-abolitionist coalition—asked the Government of Ireland in explicit terms, 'What kind of society do you want Ireland to be?' (FitzGerald & McGarry, 2016: 9). They identified criminalising sex purchase as *the* solution to the problem of prostitution in Ireland, with the added benefit of 're-balancing Ireland's history of patriarchal privilege and establishing Ireland's future among "progressive" nations like Sweden' (FitzGerald & McGarry, 2016: 9). Addressing the specially convened government Select Committee tasked with managing the consultation process around whether Ireland should change its penal code and introduce Swedish-style laws, a delegate from the National Women's Council of Ireland (NWCI) and national official coordinator of the EWL stated:

> The introduction of legislation had great potential to establish a new norm in our society which deems prostitution to be an [...] unacceptable social phenomenon and sends a strong message to future generations that it is not acceptable for women to be treated as commodities, to be bought and sold for sexual use. (Houses of the Oireachtas, 2012: 6)[10]

In the passage quoted above, the dynamic relationship between feminism and governmentality in the area of sexual politics plays out as neo-abolitionists dominate public debate about the meaning of prostitution in relations to the status of women in Ireland and Ireland's status among European nations. In such circumstances it becomes a *moving target* around the meaning of 'Irishness'. As ToRL rhetoric demonstrates, civil society's ability to invoke the meaning of national and international norms around gender and sexuality to convince, compel and even shame their governments to act in ways that they represent as being in the national interest means also that it takes on the mantel of a *sitting duck*.

---

[10] Available at: https://www.oireachtas.ie/en/debates/question/2012-01-17/345/. Accessed 28 September 2021.

Conclusion: Prostitution and Its Place in Wider Sexual Politics

The discussion in this chapter has mapped the progression of European sexual politics around prostitution. Using governmentality and biopolitics around certain populations' 'conduct of conduct', it has illustrated the throughline between how the emergence of prostitution as social 'problem' continues to permeate EU and domestic politics.

Our principle aim has been to demonstrate a link between prostitution as a policy issue and how this issue has contributed to the EU's ability to expand its competencies through norms and values around a range of ethical issues, such as women's reproductive rights, women's rights, sexual citizenship, same-sex marriage and sexual violence. Prostitution is an issue that illuminates differences about what constitutes a fundamental European value among Member States. In this way, it becomes a *moving target*. The EU continues to frame prostitution as an issue of gender equality and as one of many forms of VAW. As a result, various actors in that policy sphere tend also to frame it through structuring principles of gender equality, sexual freedom and human rights. The latter issue has played a key role in putting prostitution on the policy agenda.

This framing has coincided with the EU's identification of gender equality and women's human rights as European values. Such discourses have been absorbed in the Union's political identity and European institutions by identifying them as foundational values in the Article 2 of the Treaty of Lisbon (TFEU 2007). Therefore, these values have acquired normative authority and shape the EU's policy on a range of gender equality issues. Importantly, this change means that EU policy defines gender equality now in sexual rather than economic terms. This is a step change in policy. It puts concepts such as sexual coercion and freedom at the heart of the EU's gender equality framework 'in a way that could justify the involvement of the EU, at the same time as it is allowed to depict prostitution as a form of violence against women by presenting it as a non-choice and a form of sexual commodification' (Foret & Rubio Grundell, 2020: 11).

In the current political climate, the EU has a stronger mandate for sex trafficking due to its connections to securitisation and migration and the EU's desire to manage its borders and control migration (FitzGerald, 2010). In this way it becomes a *sitting duck* in wider policy debates. In the Treaty of Lisbon (TFEU 2007), for example, human trafficking in all its forms has become an autonomous issue in EU immigration policy and has led to the creation of one common anti-trafficking regime and the establishment of human trafficking as a Euro-crime, which places it within the EU's jurisdiction (Bressan, 2012: 139). This framing is based on the assumption that sex workers' and the mobility of geospecific populations of women is indistinguishable from sex trafficking and, therefore, it coincides with human trafficking which is a criminal offence in s Law (Scaramuzzino & Scaramuzzino, 2015).

Similarly, by reframing prostitution as VAW, the EWL challenged the EU's reticence to act, claiming that the EU had an obligation to act under Article 83 of the Treaty of Lisbon (TFEU 2007). One of the ways that the EWL strengthened their position was by invoking the issue of human trafficking for the purpose of sexual exploitation as a gender equality issue. They argued that, in order to tackle this crime, EU Member States had to harmonise their prostitution policies around unilateral criminalisation of the buyers of sex. In 2013, and in a move that mirrors strategies employed by nineteenth century reformers and feminists, the EWL tapped into the EU's desire for increased harmonisation, arguing that it lacks a united legal approach to prostitution as VAW a situation that it argues contravenes European goals and values. Pointing to the fact that the EU self-defines as a community based on the rule of law, the EWL declared, 'This issue [of violence against women and girls] cannot be left to national considerations, influenced by a profound and structural movement of antifeminist and conservative ideas'.[11]

References

Abel, G., & Fitzgerald, L. (2010). *Taking the crime out of sex work: New Zealand sex workers' fight for decriminalisation* (G. Abel & L. Fitzgerald, Eds.). Policy Press.

Allain, J. (2017). White slave traffic in international law. *Journal of Trafficking and Human Exploitation, 1*(1), 1–40.

Allwood, G. (2018). Agenda setting, agenda blocking and policy silence: Why is there no EU policy on prostitution? *Women's Studies International Forum, 69*, 126–134.

---

[11] Available at: https://www.womenlobby.org/European-Women-s-Lobby-written-statement-for-the-57th-session-of-the-Commission. Accessed 21 August 2020.

Anderson, B., & Andrijasevic, R. (2008). Sex, slaves and citizens: The politics of anti-trafficking. *Soundings, 40*(1), 135–145.
Arnberg, K., & Marklund, C. (2016). Illegally blonde: "Swedish sin" and pornography in American and Swedish imaginations, 1950–1971. In M. Larsson & E. Björklund (Eds.), *Swedish cinema and the sexual revolution: Critical essays* (pp. 185–200). McFarland.
Askola, H. (2007). *Legal responses to trafficking in women for sexual exploitation in the European Union*. Bloomsbury Publishing.
Barry, K. (1995). *The prostitution of sexuality: The global exploitation of women*. New York University Press.
Bernstein, E. (2007). The sexual politics of the "New Abolitionism". *Differences 18*(3), 128–151. https://doi.org/10.1215/10407391-2007-013
Bressan, S. (2012). Criminal law against human trafficking within the EU: A comparison of an approximated legislation. *European Journal of Crime, Criminal Law and Criminal Justice, 20*(2), 137–163.
Bristow, E. (1982). *Prostitution and prejudice: The Jewish fight against white slavery, 1870–1939*. Oxford University Press.
Carline, A., & Scoular, J. (2017). Almost abolitionism: The peculiarities of prostitution policy in England and Wales. In A. Carline, J. Scoular, E. Ward, & G. Wylie (Eds.), *Feminism, prostitution and the state* (pp. 103–120). Routledge.
Corbin, A. (1990). *Women for hire: Prostitution and sexuality in France after 1850*. Harvard University Press.
Danna, D. (2012). Client-only criminalization in the city of Stockholm: A local research on the application of the "Swedish Model" of prostitution policy. *Sexuality Research and Social Policy, 9*(1), 80–93.
Dodillet, S., & Östergren, P. (2011, March 3 and 4). *The Swedish sex purchase act: Claimed success and documented effects*. Conference paper presented at the International Workshop: Decriminalizing Prostitution and Beyond: Practical Experiences and Challenges.
Erikson, J. (2017). *Criminalising the client: Institutional change, gendered ideas and feminist strategies*. Rowman & Littlefield.
Erikson, J. (2019). An ideational approach to gendered institutional change: Revisiting the institutionalization of a new prostitution regime in Sweden. *NORA—Nordic Journal of Feminist and Gender Research, 27*(1), 22–40.
Euchner, E. M., & Engeli, I. (2018). Conflict over values in the European multilevel space: The case of morality issues. In F. Foret & O. Calligaro (Eds.), *European values: Challenges and opportunities for EU governance* (pp. 65–79). Routledge.
European Parliament. (1986). Accessed 2 December 2021.
European Parliament. (1997). *Resolution on the need to establish an EU-wide campaign for zero tolerance of violence against women*. https://op.europa.eu/

en/publication-detail/-/publication/894ae31d-35dc-48cc-9bdc-cf6fbd7d9 4ff/language-en. Accessed 20 June 2021.
European Parliament. (2004). https://www.europarl.europa.eu/doceo/doc ument/A-7-2014-0075_EN.html. Accessed 2 December 2021.
European Parliament. (2014). https://www.europarl.europa.eu/doceo/doc ument/A-7-2014-0071_EN.html. Accessed 2 December 2021.
FitzGerald, S. (2010). Biopolitics and the regulation of vulnerability: The case of the female trafficked migrant. *International Journal of Law in Context, 6*(3), 277–294.
FitzGerald, S. (2020). Trafficked women's presentation of self before the German courts. *European Journal of Women's Studies, 27*(1), 57–71.
FitzGerald, S., & McGarry, K. (2016). Problematizing prostitution in law and policy in the Republic of Ireland: A case for reframing. *Social & Legal Studies, 25*(3), 289–309.
Foret, F., & Rubio Grundell, L. (2020). European morality politics in the European Union: The case of prostitution. *Sexuality & Culture, 24*(6), 1798–1814.
Foucault, M. (1972). *The archaeology of knowledge*. Routledge.
Foucault, M. (1977). *Discipline and punish*. Pantheon Books.
Foucault, M. (1980). *The history of sexuality* (Vol. 1). Vintage.
Foucault, M. (1989). Polemics, politics, and problematizations: An interview with Michel Foucault. In P. Rabinow (Ed.), *The Foucault reader* (pp. 381–390). Pantheon.
Foucault, M. (2003). *The essential Foucault: Selections from essential works of Foucault, 1954–1984*. New Press.
Gilman, S. (1985). Black bodies, white bodies: Toward an iconography of female sexuality in late nineteenth-century art, medicine, and literature. *Critical Inquiry, 12*(1), 204–242.
Government of Sweden. (1998). Bill 1997/98:55 Kvinnofrid [Women's peace] (Fritzes 1998) 105.
Holmström, C., & Skilbrei, M.-L. (2017). The Swedish sex purchase act: Where does it stand? *Oslo Law Review, 4*(2), 82–104.
Houses of the Oireachtas. (2012). *Legislation on Prostitution*. https://www.oir eachtas.ie/en/debates/question/2012-01-17/345/. Accessed 28 September 2021.
Hubbard, P., Matthews, R., & Scoular, J. (2008). Regulating sex work in the EU: Prostitute women and the new spaces of exclusion. *Gender, Place & Culture, 15*(2), 137–152.
Jacquot, S. (2015). *Transformations in EU gender equality: From emergence to dismantling*. Springer.
Jeffreys, S. (2008). *The idea of prostitution*. Spinifex Press.

Kantola, J. (2010). *Gender and the European Union*. Macmillan International Higher Education.
Kempadoo, K. (2003). Globalising sex workers' rights. *Canadian Women's Studies*, 22(3–4), 143–150.
Kulick, D. (2003). Sex in the new Europe. The criminalization of clients and Swedish fear of penetration. *Anthropological Theory*, 3(2), 199–218.
Kulick, D. (2005). Four hundred Swedish perverts. *GLQ: A Journal of Lesbian and Gay Studies*, 11(2), 205–235.
Laite, J. (2012). *Common prostitutes and ordinary citizens: Commercial sex in London, 1885–1960*. Springer.
Lammasniemi, L. (2020). International legislation on white slavery and anti-trafficking in the early twentieth century. In J. Winderdyk & J. Jones (Eds.), *The Palgrave international handbook of human trafficking* (pp. 67–78). Palgrave Macmillan.
Le Bail, H., Giametta, C., & Rassouw, N. (2019). *What do sex workers think about the French Prostitution Act? A study on the impact of the law from 13 April 2016 against the 'prostitution system' in France*. Médecins du Monde.
Lemke, T. (2013). *Foucault, governmentality, and critique*. Routledge.
Levy, J., & Jakobsson, P. (2014). Sweden's abolitionist discourse and law: Effects on the dynamics of Swedish sex work and on the lives of Sweden's sex workers. *Criminology & Criminal Justice*, 14(5), 593–607.
MacKinnon, C. (1987). *Feminism unmodified: Discourses on life and law*. Harvard University Press.
Mathieu, L. (2004). The debate on prostitution in France: A conflict between abolitionism, regulation and prohibition. *Journal of Contemporary European Studies*, 12(2), 153–163.
Mattson, G. (2016). *The cultural politics of European prostitution reform: Governing loose women*. Springer.
Mazur, A. (2001). Republican universalism resists state feminist approaches to gendered equality in France. In A. Mazur (Ed.), *State feminism, women's movements, and job training: Making democracies work in the global economy* (pp. 155–182). Routledge.
McClintock, A. (1995). *Imperial leather: Race, gender, and sexuality in the colonial contest*. Routledge.
Olsson, N. (2021). The implementation of Sweden's prostitution law at the local level. *Journal of Social Work*, 21(3), 353–373.
Östergren, P. (2018). Sweden. In S. Jahnsen & H. Wagenaar (Eds.), *Assessing prostitution policies in Europe* (pp. 169–180). Routledge.
Outshoorn, J. (2015). The struggle for bodily integrity in the Netherlands. In J. Outshoorn (Ed.), *European women's movements and body politics: Citizenship, gender and diversity* (pp. 52–58). Palgrave Macmillan.

Outshoorn, J. (2018). European Union and prostitution policy. In S. Jahnsen & H. Wagenaar (Eds.), *Assessing prostitution policies in Europe* (pp. 363–375). Routledge.

Pliley, J. (2010). Claims to protection: The rise and fall of feminist abolitionism in the league of nations' committee on the traffic in women and children, 1919–1936. *Journal of Women's History, 22*(4), 90–113.

Pollack, M., & Hafner-Burton, E. (2000). Mainstreaming gender in the European Union. *Journal of European Public Policy, 7*(3), 432–456.

Rose, N., & Miller, P. (1992). Political power beyond the state: Problematics of government. *The British Journal of Sociology, 43*(2), 173–205.

Rose, N., O'Malley, P., & Valverde, M. (2006). Governmentality. *Annual Review of Law and Social Science, 2,* 83–104.

Rubio Grundell, L. (2021). The EU's approach to prostitution: Explaining the 'why' and 'how' of the EP's neo-abolitionist turn. *European Journal of Women's Studies. Advance Online Publication.* https://doi.org/10.1177%2F1350506821994611

Saunders, P. (2005). Traffic violations: Determining the meaning of violence in sexual trafficking versus sex work. *Journal of Interpersonal Violence, 20*(3), 343–360.

Scaramuzzino, R., & Scaramuzzino, G. (2015). Sex workers' rights movement and the EU: Challenging the new European prostitution policy model. In H. Johansson & S. Kalm (Eds.), *EU civil society: Patterns of cooperation, competition and conflict* (pp. 137–154). Palgrave Macmillan.

Scoular, J. (2015). *The subject of prostitution: Sex work, law and social theory.* Routledge.

Scoular, J., & FitzGerald, S. (2021). Why decriminalise prostitution? Because law and justice aren't always the same. *International Journal for Crime, Justice and Social Democracy, 10*(4), 52–65.

Skilbrei, M.-L. (2019). Assessing the power of prostitution policies to shift markets, attitudes, and ideologies. *Annual Review of Criminology, 2,* 493–508.

Skilbrei, M.-L., & Holmström, C. (2013). *Prostitution policies in the Nordic region: Ambiguous sympathies.* Ashgate.

Subrahmanian, R. (2009). Sexual politics and social policy: Swedish policy reviewed. In N. Kabeer & A. Stark with E. Magnus (Eds.), *Global perspectives on gender equality: Reversing the gaze* (pp. 111–135). Routledge.

Svanström, Y. (2004). Criminalising the john: A Swedish gender model? In J. Outshoorn (Ed.), *The politics of prostitution: Women's movements, democratic states and the globalisation of sex commerce* (pp. 225–244). Cambridge University Press.

Vuolajärvi, N. (2019). Governing in the name of caring—The Nordic model of prostitution and its punitive consequences for migrants who sell sex. *Sexuality Research and Social Policy, 16*(2), 151–165.
Waites, M. (2005). *Young people, sexuality and citizenship.* Palgrave.
Walkowitz, J. (1980). The politics of prostitution. *Signs: Journal of Women in Culture and Society, 6*(1), 123–135.
Ward, E., & Wylie, G. (2014). 'Reflexivities of discomfort': Researching the sex trade and sex trafficking in Ireland. *European Journal of Women's Studies, 21*(3), 251–263.
Ward, E., & Wylie, G. (2017). *Feminism, prostitution and the state: The politics of neo-abolitionism.* Routledge.
Yttergren, Å., & Westerstrand, J. (2016). The Swedish legal approach to prostitution: Trends and tendencies in the prostitution debate. *NORA-Nordic Journal of Feminist and Gender Research, 24*(1), 45–55.

CHAPTER 4

What Kind of Problematic Is Rape for the EU?

Abstract This chapter extends our analysis of European sexual politics in the context of rape vis-à-vis the EU's desire for 'ever closer union' and Members States' acceptance of or resistance to this political goal. The chapter does not focus on how the EU and its Member States regulate rape per se. But rather, it focuses on how rape has emerged as a problem of governance at the EU and Member State levels. Primarily, the chapter examines the tensions and conflicts surrounding the current 'moment' in feminist thinking around VAW generally, and around sexual violence in particular, at the EU level. Secondly, we analyse why and how rape have become implicated in the EU's desire for 'ever closer union' and in national identity politics as a form of resistance to European immorality. And finally, we map the EU hard law and soft policies on rape.

Keywords Rape · VAW · Feminism · Governance · 'The conduct of conduct' · Policy · Law

In 2013, the World Health Organisation (WHO) released a report which declared that violence against women (VAW) was 'a global health problem of epidemic proportions'.[1] Although it would be an exaggeration to state that the report falls on deaf ears, it would be accurate to claim that it does not receive widespread public attention.

Spring forward to 2017. At that time, the world seemed ready to listen. Two pieces of investigative journalism, researched and written by Jodi Kantor and Megan Twohey of *The New York Times* and Ronan Farrow in *The New Yorker*,[2] were on the pulse of the shift in public perception of the problem of sexual violence. Taken together, these reports seemed to puncture the veil of silence around sexual violence by tapping into a deep vein of untold (but well understood) accounts of women's experiences. While the reports focused on men's sexual predation in the film and entertainment industry, their framing and representation of a culture of male entitlement resonated with women's lived experiences globally (Boyle, 2019). In response, women took to social media *en mass* and, under the hash tag *#MeToo*,[3] they recounted their experiences publicly. In doing so, they invoked a long history of feminist consciousness-raising (Serisier, 2018). And while it is debatable whether this current 'moment' around sexual violence is sustainable or will result in societal or institutional change, it seems safe to say that in 2021 rape and other forms of sexual violence are meta-narratives in the public debate about gender inequality globally.

In this chapter, we use this 'moment' as a spring board to thinking critically about the wider social, cultural and normative politics that shape European sexual politics around rape. We begin our analysis by posing the following guiding question: What kind of problematic is rape for

---

[1] Available: https://apps.who.int/mediacentre/news/releases/2013/violence_aga inst_women_20130620/en/index.html. Accessed 5 September 2021.

[2] Available: https://www.nytimes.com/2017/10/05/us/harvey-weinstein-harassment-allegations.html and https://www.newyorker.com/news/news-desk/from-aggressive-ove rtures-to-sexual-assault-harvey-weinsteins-accusers-tell-their-stories. Accessed 7 September 2021.

[3] It is important to note that the *Metoo* moment predates its 2017 resurgence as *#MeToo*. Tarana Burke founded the *Metoo* movement in 2006 to demand support and recognition for young women of colour who have experienced sexual abuse. For an analysis of the classed and racialised orientation of orientation of *#MeToo*, see Gill and Orgad (2018).

the EU? In order to answer this question, we take inspiration from the literature on governmentality. In this endeavour, we are interested not in how the EU and its Member States regulate rape per se, but rather how rape 'emerges as a target for government' (Rose & Valverde, 1998). As we have discussed in Chapter 3, it is one of the key lessons of Foucault's (2003) analysis of the genealogy of the modern state that it does not achieve its legitimacy through territoriality or discipline alone. But rather, governing occurs in other ways that are located in dispersed sites, including the human body. As Golder notes: 'For Foucault, the modality proper to governing is conducting. To govern is to conduct. Government is the conduct of one's (and others') conduct, the very "conduct of conduct"' (2015: 53). We believe that we can put Foucault's theory of governmentality as the 'conduct of conduct' to new uses in our work on the European sexual politics of rape. Combined with our feminist theoretical framework, Foucault's thinking extends to our analysis of the tensions and conflicts surrounding the EU's attempts to harmonise norms and values 'by encouraging, in an infinite variety of ways' conformity on how 'the law constructs proper – even civilised – behaviour' (Stychin, 2003: 3). Yet, we argue that the road towards 'an ever closer union' expressed in the Treaty of Rome (EEC, 1957) cannot be understood as a linear progression. Rather, it is a relational process in which some Member States participate willingly and others resist what they perceive as the imposition of 'European values' around gender and sexuality on national mores (Kulpa & Mizielińska, 2011).

In this chapter, we explore the 'conduct of conduct' at the EU and domestic level around rape through two entwined conceptions of governmentality.

First, we argue that in EU Member States rape is a clear example of the normative disciplining power of the law around sexual violence (Stychin, 2003). And yet, the EU does not recognise rape as a Euro-crime. Consequently, this makes attempts to harmonise legal norms in this area very difficult (Jehle, 2012). As the EU and its Member States struggle to agree on what constitutes the crime of rape, rape becomes a *moving target* in normative debates around the meaning of gender equality at the EU and domestic levels.

Secondly, the EU's and its Member States' concern with the 'conduct of conduct' around gender and sexuality operates at other levels of governmentality 'beyond the routine theatres of state power' (Foucault, 2003: 27). Therefore, as the EU attempts to push for harmonisation across the Union, rape as a gender equality issue becomes a free-floating discourse or *sitting duck* in ideological conflicts between Brussels and certain EU Member States. It is in this way that rape is apt to be appropriated and re-appropriated strategically in the service of issues of higher political importance at the EU and domestic levels. Also, it is here that we glimpse moments of how cohesion, conflict and rupture between Brussels and nation-state politics manifest. Crucially, these are not discrete processes. But rather they are a cluster of aims, tensions, strategies, techniques of power and critical framings of gender and sexuality that sometimes work in isolation and at other times work in concert. Our discussion below considers how to understand struggles around the meaning of rape and the political instrumentalisation of rape operates at multiple levels and times.

In order to manage this complex issue, we divide this chapter into three sections. In Section One entitled: 'Positioning Rape in the EU Political Imaginary', we situate the current 'moment' in feminist thinking at the EU level around VAW generally, and around sexual violence in particular. In Section Two entitled: 'Establishing 'a European' Position on VAW' we examine why and how rape have become implicated in the 'ever closer union' of the EU. And in Section Three entitled: 'The EU's Hard and Soft Approach to VAW', we map and discuss the implications of the EU's hard law and soft policies on rape.

Positioning Rape in the EU Political Imaginary

In Europe, the feminist campaign against sexual violence has been important in the development of gender equality as a concept and a policy objective for 50 years (Edwards, 2010). Feminists working at the coal face of rape activism have been part of these political projects for a long time (Roggeband, 2021). Their political activism notwithstanding, the EU does not have a uniform law and policy position on rape (Koch et al., 2011). Instead, it defines and responds to it within the wider suite of policies around VAW (Montoya, 2013). This fixes rape in the EU law and policy imaginary as a gender-specific issue that is focused solely on the idiom of the female 'victim' of sexual assault.

Similar to other aspects of the EU gender equality framework, the EU responds to sexual violence through its obligations to establish gender equality via its obligation to prevent discrimination in the workplace (Ahrens, 2019). This arises from the EU's use of the Committee on the Elimination of Discrimination against Women (CEDAW) definition of VAW as a form of discrimination established in its General Recommendation established in 1992 (Edwards, 2010). Critics, however, challenge the EU's use of this definition on several grounds.

First, they argue that it demonstrates the EU's failure to take VAW seriously in general, and rape in particular, especially relative to how it prioritises an understanding of rape as 'discriminatory' rather than as a form of 'violence' (Anthias, 2014). This creates a situation, they claim, where the EU's use of this definition conflates a broad range of acts and situations that, in other circumstances, the authorities would normally address separately such as sexual, physical and psychological or emotional violence. This supports the critique that applying a discrimination perspective to rape, instead of seeing it as related to gender equality and as a form of gendered violence, situates its causes, harms and solutions at the level of the individual, instead of looking to structural, societal and cultural explanations and remedies (Jacquot, 2015).

Secondly, they argue that this way of framing the issue addresses sexual violence and other gendered harms only when they are committed against women (Walby et al., 2017). This tunnel vision eschews the vast scholarship that demonstrates that this definition is heteronormative because it concentrates on men's violence against women alone (Roseneil et al., 2013).

Thirdly, they argue that this usage conflates diverse acts that occur for a variety of reasons, and not only due to gender relations in society (Askola, 2007). Thus, conflating femicide and consensual prostitution, for example, fails to recognise the significant differences that exist between these phenomena (Carline, 2011).

And finally, critics point to the fact that rape is not always included in the EU's definition of VAW (Vázquez et al., 2021).

These critiques are not unique to EU's understanding of rape. A cursory glance at a selection of jurisdictions will show that their legal systems respond to rape differently. For example, in the US the question of how colleges and universities react to incidents of rape on their campuses is hotly debated among feminists, politicians and society in general (Harris, 2019). It is well-known that the US implements draconian punishments, instead of policies to address the underlying issues of social inequality, gender relations and racism driving this issue (Gruber, 2020). In comparison, EU countries are far less punitive in their approach. Europe is a diverse continent socially, culturally and politically.

Crucially, and particularly in terms of our argument in this book, European jurisdictions differ around which acts they recognise as constituting rape (e.g. whether they include anal and oral penetration and whether the core requirement is the use of force or lack of consent) (Dünkel, 2017). Such differences have consequences for the levels of reported cases of rape in each jurisdiction. Countries with a low threshold for counting an act as constituting force or lack of consent as rape tend to register more incidents (Humbert et al., 2021). For example, Sweden is a good example of a jurisdiction with a low threshold and broad definition of what constitutes rape. This, together with the fact that the government is actively encouraging complainants to report to the authorities, means that registered figures are higher than in many other jurisdictions without indicating that rape is more prevalent in Sweden than elsewhere (see e.g., The Swedish National Council for Crime Prevention, 2020). In what follows, we want to examine how the EU has taken up the discourse of rape as a gender equality issue by honing in on how it understands and attempts to regulate sexual violence generally, and rape specifically.

As we described in Chapter 2, the EU's engagement with gender equality has been driven by its economic rationalities (Sümer, 2009). Consequently, it has instrumentalised gender equality to serve its policy goals outside gender justice (Lombardo & Meier, 2008). Yet, here it is useful to return to Foucault's (2003) theory of governmentality to illuminate how rape as a gender equality issue has become a *moving target* in European sexual politics. In the context of the EU's desire to harmonise the 'conduct of conduct' around European identity, we can trace how the EU has instrumentalised VAW as a discourse for meaning-making which, in turn, it uses to regulate whether current and prospective members are 'good' or 'bad' Europeans measured against whether the EU considers them to be dedicated enough to prescribed gender and sexuality norms and values (Ignjatović & Bošković, 2013; Sedef, 2010).

In situations such as these, tensions around VAW generally and rape more specifically have the potential to derail the European project. Due to the large and diverse nature of European societies, a variety of social norms and values that structure individual nations' attitudes to rape and other forms of sexual violence coexist. This means that gender and sexuality have also become sites of resistance to the EU (Buyantueva & Shevtsova, 2019). While the EU sits as both judge and jury on what counts as gender equality across the Union, we must also consider the fact that the EU is itself often the object of criticism on its perceived inability to develop and implement policies that can transform gender relations and secure sexual rights for all (Cavaghan, 2017; Smith & Villa, 2010; Stratigaki, 2005).

Feminists criticise the EU for not making VAW core to its gender equality policies (Walby, 2004). This links to the larger feminist critique that in EU institutions gender equality has become something that supports technocratic accountability rather than contributing to fundamental shifts in gender relations (Cullen, 2015; FitzGerald & Freedman, 2021). They claim that gender mainstreaming depoliticises feminist thinking on gender equality in many areas because the EU focuses on the 'big picture' rather than on the specificities that make gender inequality so pervasive (Squires, 2005). Counter to the EU's technocratic approach to gender equality, feminist engagement with sexual violence directs our attention to the structural inequalities and gender and sexuality discourses that consistently disadvantage women and support patriarchy (Lombardo & Verloo, 2009). For them, VAW is 'neither random nor individual' (MacKinnon, 1993: 25). Therefore, in order to combat rape they argue that it will require social and normative change at multiple levels rather than the EU's preference for technocratic solutions that facilitate its political agenda only.

As we discussed in Chapter 3, EU law and policy makers focus on prostitution not as a societal issue around the racialised and gendered dimensions of poverty and marginalisation, but rather for its connections to human trafficking. In the case of rape, however, it is less clear how rape came to figure in the EU policy realm. As we indicate above, the EU continues to view criminal matters in Member States' jurisdictions to be outside its competence. And yet, criminal law, and particularly rape law, is a key site for governmental regulation of the sexual relations between citizens and between the EU and its Member States (Du Toit, 2007: 61). Although sexual violence has historically been a matter for domestic legal regimes to address, as the EU has expanded its *acquis communautaire* to support an ever closer union, this has brought VAW within its scope of influence (Choudhry, 2016). Today, this agenda is embedded institutionally at the EU level due to public and private efforts in all layers of governance (Montoya, 2013). As a consequence when the EU attempts to harmonise fundamental principles across the Union, this has created a situation that enhances its biopolitical regulation of European citizens.

Feminist research on rape law in the last 20–30 years shows that European jurisdictions have been active in revising their penal codes, and have introduced new legislation to address sexual violence (Nevala,

2017; Siegel, 2020). Overall, we can see that the threshold for minimum punishment for sexual violence has increased in Western European jurisdictions (Dünkel, 2017). Embedded in European sexual politics around rape are two competing frames that encode sexual violence with meaning in normative terms. We want to consider these frames because they are core to how law and policy at the EU and domestic levels respond to rape. But, also, we want to do this because these frames provide interesting examples of the operation of the 'micro powers' of governmentality underpinning law and policy debates around rape (Foucault, 2003: 192).

Interestingly, the two policy areas of this book, prostitution and rape, are different in the sense that while prostitution as a matter of criminal law is controversial, there is agreement that rape is a heinous crime that must be prohibited by means of the criminal law throughout the Union. Yet, disagreements remain about how law should be define it and, thus, where the boundary should be between rape and 'just sex', to use Cahill's term (2014). Today, in the EU, the main fault line exists between those jurisdictions which define rape as 'coerced acts' and those that define it as an act undertaken in the 'absence of consent' (Munro, 2017). We do not suggest that one legal model is superior to the other. It is beyond the scope of this book to delve into the intricacies of the criminal law and criminal procedure in different jurisdictions around coercion and absence of consent in rape. But it is useful, however, to make the following observations about the distinctions between both approaches.

Feminist researchers demonstrate that in jurisdictions where consent-based rape laws have been in place for a long time, such as the Republic of Ireland, normative discourse and practice often shifts attention away from the perpetrator to the complainant (Leahy, 2014). By contrast, in jurisdictions where the law defines rape as coerced sex, such as France, then the court must take the defendant's actions into consideration and evaluate whether or not these actions meet the standard of proof for coercion. Thus, consentbased rape laws require that the court hear evidence of whether the defendant could have interpreted the complainant's actions *as consent*. In such contexts, what the court can interpret as reasonable indications that a woman wants sex become relevant. Crucially, this gives the perpetrator scope to argue that the defendant could have interpreted what the complainant did or said as consent to sex. Consequently, it is the complainant who in reality stands trial and not the defendant (Munro, 2010). To get some purchase on why this is important requires grappling with the vestiges of a culture of rape in Europe and elsewhere that make it difficult to prosecute this crime (McGlynn & Munro, 2010). This difficulty emerged in contexts, in which historically the courts did not recognise non-consensual sex taking place, within a marriage as rape. Rape legislation is historically linked to morality, infidelity and men's ownership over women's sexuality, and in some instances, the language of vice and immorality has been retained in the criminal law provisions. As we will discuss below, in certain EU nations the vestiges of this discursive frame and its normative potential to manage the 'conduct of conduct' of citizens, and particularly women's bodies and behaviours, have become ripe with meaning and fertile ground for forms of biopolitical governmentality expressed in national identity politics and resistance to European values. Putting that idea to one side for now but we will return to it later, in the next section we turn to how the EU has established on rape via its take on VAW.

Establishing 'A European' Position on VAW

The protection of women from gender-based violence is neither enshrined in EU treaties nor the EU Charter of Fundamental Human Rights (2000). Initially, the EU mentioned VAW in Article 1 (TFEU, 1957), which provided that among 'the efforts to eradicate inequalities between women and men the Union will aim to combat all forms of domestic violence in different policy areas'. For a long time, this was the only reference to VAW in the EU *acquis*. As we discussed in Chapter 3, this began to change when the European Parliament (EP) proposed the *resolution on violence against women* (1986).[4] In the intervening years until 2014, however, EU policy in this area was located primarily in soft policies, such as Council Conclusions, Parliament Resolutions and Commission Strategies.

So far in this chapter we have addressed the EU's framing of VAW as a gender equality issue in the Union. Within that normative ecosystem, some doleful facts emerge that open up the world around governmentality through the 'conduct of conduct' of geo-specific populations' bodies and behaviours relative to VAW. Foucault places the question of the connections between 'populations' and the 'conduct of conduct' at the centre of 'forms of normalisation peculiar to security' (2009: 397). By broadening

---

[4] Available at: https://www.europarl.europa.eu/EPRS/PE2_AP_RP!FEMM.1984_A2-0044!860001EN.pdf. Accessed 24 April 2021.

out the application of his theorisation in this volume, his thinking directs us to new conceptual spaces where our focus tends towards how the EU extends its power beyond territory and ideology, and takes us into the discursive spaces around European identity-formation. This socio-spatial reading of governmentality helps us to unpack some other processes at play where EU policy on VAW interacts with discourses on 'race'.

We find evidence of the emergence of a racialised discourse in the EP's Resolutions around VAW. In ways that reflect governmentality as the racialised form of social control of the European body politic, we suggest that it is possible to identify how the EU instrumentalises the issue of VAW as a biopolitical strategy in a wider discourse, in which the EU, its values and its peoples are a 'society that must be defended' (Foucault, 2003). We can illuminate this dynamic by returning to geopolitical events in Europe at the turn of the millennium.

At this time, Europe began to experience the effects of processes of globalisation through mass migration from former Soviet Bloc countries and the Global South. The EU and its Member States responded to this situation by introducing stricter border and immigration controls which they articulated through discourses of securitisation to defend 'Fortress Europe' (FitzGerald, 2008). As Europe began to close its borders to protect its body politic, another portal opened onto a discursive space, in which the EU weaved racialised assumptions about 'other' cultures' attitudes to gender and sexuality into its justifications for its exclusionary policy decisions. As Montoya and Rolandsen Agustín observe, in that context VAW emerges less as a 'domestic' and pervasive problem in social relations, and more as inextricably linked to 'other' cultures' attitudes to gender and sexuality that are diametrically opposed to 'European' gender equality and anti-violence values (2013: 535). Distilled into this racialised discourse and grounded in a policy of securitisation, the combination of gender and sexuality norms and values contained within EU level initiatives point to a different politics at play. Represented as paradigmatic of women's larger oppression, VAW facilities the entry onto discourse of the most blatant example of biopolitical governmentality. In short, we witness how perceived rather than actual cultural differences become racialised tactics to distinguish between a European identity and all 'others' (Kantola, 2010).

On the one hand, the discourses around VAW make it into a *moving target* in disputes around the meaning of a European identity. On the other hand, and as we will discuss below, these racialised discourses have significance as they become *sitting ducks* or proxies in wider debates about European identity *vis-à-vis* national identity politics that are articulated in debates around 'what' and 'who' is 'out of place' in Europe.

As the EU expanded its jurisdiction to include aspects of citizens' public and private lives, it continued to refrain from addressing VAW directly:

> [T]he adoption of the Maastricht Treaty, with its pillar devoted to Justice and Home Affairs issues, created the political space for a new and vigorous EU policy on violence against women, and area previously off-limits to the economically orientated EC. (Pollack & Hafner-Burton, 2000: 434)

Later, the EU adopted the Treaty of Amsterdam (EC, 1997) which established the legal basis for wider EU policy reform around VAW. It did this by emphasising VAW as a human rights issue (Pollack & Hafner-Burton, 2000). It is important to note that these developments coincide with international developments that are linked to a series of world conferences on human rights.

First, the United Nations Human Rights High Commission (UNHRC) adopted the Vienna Declaration and Programme of Action (VDPA) at the World Conference on Human Rights in Vienna in 1993. PART 11, paragraph 18 of the VDPA highlights the importance of 'women's rights' and the rights of the 'girl child'. The VDPA recognises gender-based violence, sexual harassment and exploitation as issues for the international community. Crucially, Part III paragraph 38 of the VDPA calls upon the UN General Assembly to adopt the draft UN Declaration on the Elimination of Violence against Women (DEVAW, 1993).[5] It encourages states to combat VAW in accordance with the provisions set out in the Declaration, which identifies rape as an issue 'requiring an effective response' (DEVAW, 1993).

Secondly, the Commission on the Status of Women organised a series of conferences on women. Of these, the Fourth World Conference on Women in Beijing in 1995 is noteworthy. At this conference, the international community agreed on a comprehensive plan to achieve global

---

[5] Available at: https://www.ohchr.org/en/professionalinterest/pages/violenceagainstwomen.aspx. Accessed 24 April 2021.

legal equality, namely the Beijing Platform for Action.[6] To date, the Platform remains a blueprint for advancing women's rights by using gender mainstreaming as a tool to promote gender equality. The document includes three strategic objectives on VAW, namely to: (1): 'Take integrated measures to prevent and eliminate violence against women'; (2): 'Study the causes and consequences of violence against women and the effectiveness of preventative measures'; and (3): 'Eliminate trafficking in women and assist victims of violence due to prostitution and trafficking'. In 1996, the EU adopted the Platform as an expression of its formal commitment to gender mainstreaming, and as a basis for gender equality policy and the eradication of all forms of gender-based violence (Walby, 2005).

We can also analyse the EU's response to VAW and its adoption of the Beijing Declaration (1995) in terms of the 'micro-politics' underpinning 'the institutional developments in the late 1990s that contributed to the expansion of EU equality policies by creating more favourable political structures for women's policy demands' (Mazey, 2000: 11). In practice, this meant that as the EU implicated VAW in its push for greater harmonisation on policy across the Union, a political space emerged where coalitions of feminists, academics, activists, femocrats and politicians could engage in agenda-setting through the ecosystem of VAW.

As we mentioned earlier, the way in which the EU created its policies is related to the emergence of an opportunity structure or what have come to be defined as 'epistemic communities'. Haas (2015) finds these communities' main characteristics to be that they share a normative foundation, that they build on an assumption of causality between practices and outcomes, that they share a position on what knowledge and expertise should count and they share a common goal. Applied to our case in this chapter, we see experts as the embodiment of governmentality as they come together across the EU/Member State and private/public divides to address and solve the problem of rape based on a shared understanding of gender inequality. Ultimately for them a shared understanding of rape and gender equality is the solution. While we do not apply epistemic communities as a comprehensive approach in our analysis in this book, we share an interest in the 'process through which consensus is reached within a given domain of expertise and through which the consensual

---

[6] Available at: https://www.ohchr.org/EN/Issues/Women/SRWomen/Pages/BeijingPlatformforAction.aspx. Accessed 24 April 2021.

knowledge is diffused to and carried forward by other actors' (Haas, 2015: 23).

Exploring these micro-politics of governmentality around feminist engagement with EU policy on VAW, we are drawn immediately to how events occurring within the Union in 1995 around enlargement shape this policy process. As we saw in Chapter 3, researchers have suggested that Sweden's accession to the EU has produced the so-called 'Scandinavian effect' in its policy sphere. Put simply, Sweden's accession to the EU resulted in a particular kind of feminist civil society actors taking their place in its policymaking fora. These actors came to the EU armed with the firm belief that VAW was a gender equality issue (Pollack & Hafner-Burton, 2000). Such was the power of their conviction that over time it changed the tone and tenor of the debate on VAW at the EU level. We submit that governmentality is a key concept that can help us to understand how the 'Scandinavian effect' contributed to the 'production of knowledge' and the 'conduct of conduct' around VAW at the EU level.

We find evidence of the transference of this geo-specific feminist understanding of VAW in how women's organisations have lobbied the EU to take VAW seriously as a universal human rights issue, and to make VAW one of its political and legislative priorities (Joachim, 2007). As part of this campaign, women's organisations re-doubled their efforts to get VAW on the EU's political agenda. As feminists strengthened their coalitions and defined their objectives, they succeeded in securing the EP and the European Commission (hereafter the Commission) involvement in the 'Campaign for Zero Tolerance for Violence Against Women' (1997).[7] At its core we can detect the hallmarks of Swedish strategies in the campaign. For example, the campaign identified public awareness, better prevention and the elimination of all forms of violence as key objectives. In support of this policy direction, the Treaty of Amsterdam (EC, 1997) incorporated gender mainstreaming within EU equality law, and made gender equality 'an essential task of the EU' (Articles 2 and 3[2]). Over the coming years, the EU adopted several Resolutions and Recommendations designed to further this agenda. Examples include, the Resolution

---

[7] Available at: https://op.europa.eu/en/publication-detail/-/publication/894ae31d-35dc-48cc-9bdc-cf6fbd7d94ff/language-en. Accessed 20 June 2021.

on trafficking of women (2000),[8] the Resolution *on the elimination of honour crimes against women*, the Recommendation *on combating violence against women* (2006) and the *Resolution on the Elimination of Violence Against Women* (2009).[9]

Going into the substance of feminists' role in this campaign, we note how their discourse and practice take on the hew of governmentality through their participation in the 'conduct of conduct'. Key is their ability to position themselves in the EU policy sphere through 'the production of knowledge' and by offering expertise around the conceptualisation and implementation of policy on VAW as a gender equality issue (FitzGerald & Freedman, 2021). In their hands, the meaning of VAW as a gender equality issue becomes a *moving target* in the furtherance of their specific political agenda. As Kutay observes, feminist institutionalise their version of gender equality by 'governing with knowledge' (2014: 27). This process is neither value nor politically neutral. But rather only those who can demonstrate that they are aligned with the hegemonic meaning and EU's political agenda will receive recognition. In return, those aligned voices will provide the EU with the gender credibility it lacks. Therefore, in the area of rape, women's organisations have a vested interest in governing through the 'conduct of conduct' in ways that support the EU's desired normative 'European identity' (Seibicke, 2020).

Feminist involvement in agenda-setting at the EU level has opened up a space where women's organisations can pursue their justice claims. They can build coalitions and work to get particular issues on the political agenda. This is important for those women's groups whose political contexts 'at home' stymie or silence all discussion on issues around gender and sexuality. This activity, however, can bring them into direct conflict with their governments' official stance. Thus, national resistance to the EU's soft law policies to encourage nations to address VAW, including rape, for example, can become a *sitting duck* between national actors, national governments and the EU as each jockey for political recognition. As Wylie (2016) observes, in certain Eastern European contexts resistance to 'Europeanness' around gender and sexuality

---

[8] Available at: https://www.europarl.europa.eu/sides/getDoc.do?pubRef=-//EP//TEXT+TA+P5-TA-2000-0248+0+DOC+XML+V0//EN. Accessed 20 June 2021.

[9] Available at: https://www.europarl.europa.eu/doceo/document/TA-6-2006-0038_EN.html and https://www.europarl.europa.eu/doceo/document/TA-7-2009-0098_EN.html. Accessed 20 June 2021.

serves as evidence of patriotism. As we will discuss in more detail in Chapter 5, in Poland, for example, resistance to EU norms and values around sexual violence is enmeshed in right wing politics. In that context, proponents of that political view use their rejection of European 'perversity' to demonstrate their commitment to protecting 'real European values' (Kajta, 2017). Viewed thus, conservative values and the need to regulate citizens' sexual behaviour are core European values. Therefore, in those jurisdictions resistance to EU gender and sexuality norms around rape and other forms of VAW are taken up and articulated as evidence of protecting Europeanness and not threatening it.

In this final section of this chapter, we look at the political rationalities and governance technologies of various EU institutions, actors and key instruments governing its stance on VAW.

The EU's Hard and Soft Approach to VAW

Seeing political rationality and governmental technologies (Rose & Miller, 1992) as two sides of the same coin, makes its necessary to explore how the political rationality of gender equality manifests in and is formed by the governmental technologies available to the EU. The rationality we outline above, builds upon discrete understandings of rape that conveys meaning about those who are to be governed by hard law and soft policies around rape. Thus, as political rationalities they are both *moving targets* and *sitting ducks* and often at the same time. This is the case for three reasons. First, political rationalities are fundamentally normative because they express the norms upon which political rationality is forged. Secondly, they are epistemological because they build upon particular normative understandings. And finally, they are conceptual because it is through conceptualisations that these norms enter public discourse (Rose & Miller, 1992). VAW, in this way, becomes a political rationality because it comprises an idea about why the EU should combat it (it is a form of gender discrimination), why it exists (due to lack of gender equality) and how it should be codified ('VAW' becomes an idiom or logic). Viewed thus, the political rationality of VAW in the EU becomes actionable in 'the complex assemblage of diverse forces' (Rose & Miller, 1992: 183).

Taking this notion of governmentally as a complex assemblage of diverse forces and applying to our context is an interesting exercise. For example, the EU has created its VAW policies and discourses in the

Commission, the Council and the EP. In order to explore this process we want to focus on the Commission because it is the EU's most important law and policy making body (Montoya & Rolandsen Agustín, 2013).

The Commission addresses VAW by focusing on gender equality. For example, it devised the *Community Action Programme on equal opportunities in the area of labour market policies between men and women 1991–1995* (COM[90]449) and 1996–2000 (COM[95]381). Later, it introduced the 2001–2005 *Programme* (COM[2000]335),[10] which identifies the fight against gender-related violence and human trafficking as operational objectives relative to structural gender inequalities. As the Commission began to engage more with gender equality, it introduced the *2006–2010 Roadmap for Equality between Women and Men* (COM[2006]92).[11] The roadmap identifies six priority areas for EU action on gender equality. It identifies the 'eradication of all forms of gender-based violence' as a priority area. This policy direction indicates the Commission's decision to take a more active role in combatting VAW. While this is one of the EU's goals, it is interesting to note that in ways that mirror racialised 'othering' we discussed in the previous section, the Commission stresses the need 'for urgent action … to eliminate customary or traditional harmful attitudes and practices, including female mutilation, early and forced marriages and honour crimes' (quoted in Montoya & Rolandsen Agustín, 2013: 550). More recently, the Commission published a second *Strategy for Equality between Women and Men (2010–2015)* (COM[2010]491 final),[12] which incorporated a wider definition of gendered violence but with a particular emphasis on female genital mutilation (FGM).

By contrast, the Commission's *EU Guidelines on VAW and Girls Combatting all forms of Discrimination against Them* (2008)[13] is a

---

[10] Available at: https://www.euromed-justice.eu/en/system/files/20090428174714_COM%282000%29335final.CommunityFrameworkStrategyonGenderEquality.pdf. Accessed 24 April 2021.

[11] Available at: https://eur-lex.europa.eu/legal-content/EN/TXT/?uri=LEGISSUM%3Ac10404. Accessed 20 June 2021.

[12] Available at: https://eur-lex.europa.eu/legal-content/EN/ALL/?uri=celex%3A52010DC0491. Accessed 20 June 2021.

[13] Available at: https://ec.europa.eu/anti-trafficking/publications/eu-guidelines-violence-against-women-and-girls-and-combating-all-forms-discrimination_en. Accessed 20 June 2021.

comprehensive and multi-lateral *acquis*. The Commission identifies these guidelines as a way for the EU to take 'effective action against one of the major human rights violations of today's world'. Again, this document identifies many forms of VAW and is explicit in establishing guidelines to 'encourage' the 'implementation of a greater number of specific projects aimed at women and girls'. It references a large international legal framework and states' obligations in combatting VAW, and it includes a wide variety of definitions of VAW. In ways that resonate with our previous discussion on EU policy on VAW that are filtered through the lens of 'cultural differences', we find it of particular interest how the EU uses governmentality through the 'conduct of conduct' to regulate the composition of the EU body politic. Notably, the guidelines are focused on the EU's external policy. Rather than applying the standards laid out in this extensive document on Member States, the Guidelines are for countries outside the EU.

The establishment of 'best practice' and 'benchmarks' are key ingredients in how the EU steers policy development in its Member States. It produces comparative reports and other documentation to influence Member States' decisions in this area, in addition to providing a knowledge base for EU bodies. One such example is the Report entitled: Exploring Best Practice in Combatting Violence Against Women: Sweden, which was published by the Policy Directorate for Citizens' Rights and Constitutional Affairs for the FEMM Committee in 2018. The rationale for producing this in-depth report about Swedish policies is that Sweden is 'a country known for its exemplary work towards gender equality' (2018: 7). Failure to adhere to these 'Swedish standards' may result in sanctions from the EU and affect Member States standing within the European community normatively and socially. As Montoya (2013) reminds us, while the explicit aim of benchmarking and similar technologies is to enhance learning across the Union, they may also serve the function of being discrete coercive manoeuvres to distinguish between 'us' and them' in the hierarchy of European nations.

This brings us to the *Daphne Programme*, which is the EU's foremost policy tool for combatting VAW. Established in 1998, the programme dedicates over half of its initiatives to addressing gendered violence. We argue that this is a good example of the EU's use of capacity building to reach its normative and social goals (Montoya & Rolandsen Agustín, 2013). In 2007, however, the Commission introduced a policy change which resulted in a new framing of violence that bifurcated violence into 'widespread domestic violence' and 'traditional' forms of violence. This shift permeated down to the Daphne programme. Again, it is possible to argue that such framing activities have racialised dimensions because they have disciplining powers that regulate the composition of the EU body politic. For example, in order to become a member of the EU, candidate countries must adopt the EU *acquis* into domestic policy. Although VAW was not an integral part of the initial accession negotiation process between the Commission and candidate states, it has been increasingly included in the yearly monitoring process that is a part of the accession process. For example, a 2006 Parliament Resolution *on the current situation in combating vaw and any future action*[14] calls for the Commission to monitor VAW closely in acceding countries. At a deeper level, culture-based conceptualisations of VAW are racially coded and play a role in the monitoring process around what and who is 'in place here'. Importantly, this demonstrates how the discursive construction of Europeanness (within the monitoring process but also elsewhere) becomes a *moving target* around the meaning of the 'conduct of conduct' that determines how nations become 'European', and a *sitting duck* that is used in racialised ways to delimit the borders of 'Europeanness'.

This brings us to the most important development in the EU's response to VAW, namely the Istanbul Convention (2011). In May 2011, the Council of Europe[15] opened its Convention on Preventing and Combating Violence against Women and Domestic Violence (the Istanbul Convention) (2011) for signature and ratification by Members and non-Members of the Council of Europe, including the EU.[16] Following ten ratifications, the Convention came into force in August 2014. In 2017, the EU adopted the Istanbul Convention. The Convention is the first legally binding instrument on VAW and, as such, it constitutes an inflection point in the EU's ability to harmonise norms and values as dedicated European responses to sexual violence, including rape. Importantly, the Convention aims at violence prevention, victim protection and 'to end

---

[14] Available at: https://op.europa.eu/en/publication-detail/-/publication/7347cefd-397e-4622-8820-f99c0a07b2a7/language-en. Accessed 20 June 2021.

[15] The Council of Europe is autonomous from the EU and is a European political organisation currently with 47 member states. Its foundation is based on the principles of the European Convention in Human Rights (ECHR).

[16] Available at: https://www.coe.int/en/web/istanbul-convention/text-of-the-convention.

with the impunity of perpetrators'. Article 40 of the Explanatory Report of the Convention defines sexual harassment as 'any verbal, non-verbal and physical conduct of a sexual nature, carried out in a context of abuse of power, promise of reward or threat of reprisal, not limited to the field of employment'. Importantly, the Convention establishes a legally binding definition of VAW as 'a violation of human rights and a form of discrimination against women' and requests signatory states to criminalise VAW, including sexual violence. In this way, the Convention draws international norms developed in the European context via the European Convention on Human Rights (2000) that interprets sexual harassment as an infringement of the individual's right to freedom of expression and to a private life (Marshall, 2009).[17]

The Convention is the product of an extended process of lobbying to place VAW on the international agenda, and an increasing awareness of the extent of the problem in Europe.[18] Taking inspiration from international legal instruments, international and regional tribunals and feminist theories, the Convention makes the public/private distinction, which previously prevented States from interfering in the private sphere, irrelevant (Chinkin, 1999). The Preamble to the Convention states that VAW is the result of 'historically unequal power relations between women and men'. It identifies the 'structural' form violence takes. This means that it recognises that VAW is rooted in social relations and that it must be eliminated at that level.

What distinguishes the Convention from earlier legal instruments is that it differentiates between VAW and domestic violence, which may affect a range of individuals irrespective of gender. Article 3a of the Preamble to the Convention[19] defines VAW as, 'all acts of gender-based violence that result in, or are likely to result in, physical, sexual, psychological or economic harm or suffering to women, including threats of such acts, coercion or arbitrary deprivation of liberty, whether occurring

---

[17] For example, the UN Resolution on domestic violence available here: https://documents-dds-ny.un.org/doc/UNDOC/GEN/N03/503/40/PDF/N0350340.pdf?OpenElement.

[18] Recommendations Rec (2002) of the Committee of Ministers to Member States on the protections of women and children against violence, adopted by the Committee of Ministers of 30 April 2002 at 794th meeting of the minsters' deputies.

[19] Available at: https://eur-lex.europa.eu/legal-content/EN/TXT/HTML/?uri=CELEX:52016PC0109. Accessed 20 June 2021.

in public or in private life'. The Convention requires State Parties to criminalise several behaviours, which constitute VAW and domestic violence irrespective of whether or not these behaviours are included in domestic legal regimes' criminal codes. Such behaviours include forced marriage and sexual violence. The Convention requires that states take legislative or other measures necessary to ensure that offences established in the Convention, 'are punishable by effective, proportionate and dissuasive sanctions' (Art 45). Therefore, the Convention fills a normative gap in Europe (De Vido, 2017).

Feminists have been at the forefront of efforts to encourage the EU to adopt the Convention. As we have highlighted previously, the European Women's Lobby (EWL) is one of the most powerful women's groups that has achieved institutional recognition at the EU level. In the main, the EU has encouraged and supported their activities in this area. The EWL fights to end all form of what they term VAWG (Violence Against Women and Girls). It has pursued its objectives by tasking its national representatives with lobbying their respective governments to sign and ratify the Istanbul Convention and its monitoring mechanisms by 2020. In terms that speak to our interests, the EWL applies a broad definition of 'male violence against women' that encompass everything from harassment to murder. It does not tend to address rape as a discrete form of gender-based or sexual violence. One of the few instances where the EWL mentions rape specifically occurs within the framework of the 'ACT AGAINST RAPE! USE THE ISTANBUL CONVENTION!' project.[20] The project's main aim was to initiate dialogue at the national and European level to promote the Istanbul Convention.

While there is significant support for the Istanbul Convention throughout Europe, and while powerful actors like the EWL back it, the implementation process and some of its foundational principles have created political and cultural ripples across the Union. We will address some of these issues in Chapter 5.

---

[20] Available at: https://www.womenlobby.org/IMG/pdf/ewl_public_report_act_aga inst_rape_20140425.pdf. Accessed 28 August 2021.

Conclusion: Rethinking EU Responses to Sexual Violence

The EU's concern with sexual violence, including rape, is far from straightforward. We have argued in this chapter, that the EU's concern with sexual harassment has used gender and sexual discourses as proxies to expand its power through governing through the 'conduct of conduct'. While it is important to acknowledge that the shift from seeing sexual harassment as an act where an individual is subjected to an abuse of power in the work place, to being about sexuality and gender relations, is the first important step in getting the EU involved in the fight against sexual violence. We submit that in terms of European sexual politics in the context of rape, the EU's VAW agenda has moved its regulatory 'gaze' beyond European market relations and the protection of workers by making it possible for it to move into the realm of sexuality.

Still, when we consider the sociological implications of this frame, then we find that it is possible to grasp other more troubling processes at play that have less to do with gender equality and more to do with protecting the EU market, ensuring a constant supply of labour and to increase its competitiveness internationally (Repo, 2016; van der Vleuten, 2007; Walby, 2004), or as Liebfried says about EU's social policy generally: 'The EU's social dimension is often advocated as a corrective to market-building, but its practice seems to have been part of it' (2015: 278).

As we have argued throughout this chapter, governmentality is a useful lens to understand how VAW, and especially rape, has become implicated in the European project. In order to address this complex process, we have focused on how EU policy in this area invokes and deploys racialised and gendered discourses to define what it means to be European, and to delimit who has access to the body politic. Therefore, one of our key contributions to this conversation is the observation that while the EU sanctions Member States and prospective Member States for engaging in malpractice around gender and sexuality, it is at the same time using similar tactics to pursue a racialised politics based on the principle of 'society must be defended'. As we have discussed in this chapter, certain feminists working at the centres of EU power and decision-making have been at the forefront of this activity. And while their work to encourage the EU to sign, ratify and adopt the Istanbul Convention is to be lauded and is a vital step in holding the state at the supra and national level to account for the protection of individuals from violence. This requires a continued feminist critique because, as we have shown, the politics of the velvet triangle, including the EWL and the FEMM Committee, are not necessarily inclusive or intersectional politics that pursue justice for all. In short, their continued uncritical appeals to the law to solve the problem of rape and other forms of sexual violence eschew the fact that for many women, and particularly marginalised women, law is a blunt instrument and, as a result, it might never be able to deliver the justice victims of rape seek (Gruber, 2020).

The next chapter takes up this question at a more empirical level, situating EU law and policy around gender and sexuality in the relationships between Brussels and four EU Member States.

References

Ahrens, P. (2019). The birth, life, and death of policy instruments: 35 years of EU gender equality policy programmes. *West European Politics, 42*(1), 45–66.

Anthias, F. (2014). The intersections of class, gender, sexuality and 'race': The political economy of gendered violence. *International Journal of Politics, Culture, and Society, 27*(2), 153–171.

Askola, H. (2007). Violence against women, trafficking, and migration in the European Union. *European Law Journal, 13*(2), 204–217.

Boyle, K. (2019). What's in a name? Theorising the inter-relationships of gender and violence. *Feminist Theory, 20*(1), 19–36.

Buyantueva, R., & Shevtsova, M. (2019). Introduction: LGBTQ+ activism and the power of locals. In R. Buyantueva & M. Shevtsova (Eds.), *LGBTQ+ activism in central and eastern Europe: Resistance, representation and identity* (pp. 1–19). Palgrave Macmillan.

Cahill, A. J. (2014). Recognition, desire, and unjust sex. *Hypatia, 29*(2), 303–319.

Carline, A. (2011). Constructing the subject of prostitution: A Butlerian reading of the regulation of sex work. *International Journal for the Semiotics of Law-Revue internationale de Sémiotique juridique, 24*(1), 61–78.

Cavaghan, R. (2017). The gender politics of EU economic policy: Policy shifts and contestations before and after the crisis. In J. Kantola & E. Lombardo (Eds.), *Gender and the economic crisis in Europe* (pp. 49–71). Palgrave Macmillan.

Chinkin, C. (1999). A critique of the public/private dimension. *European Journal of International Law, 10*(2), 387–395.

Choudhry, S. (2016). Towards a transformative conceptualisation of violence against women-A critical frame analysis of council of Europe discourse on violence against women. *The Modern Law Review, 79*(3), 406–441.

Cullen, P. (2015). Feminist NGOs and the European Union: Contracting opportunities and strategic response. *Social Movement Studies, 14*(4), 410–426.

De Vido, S. (2017). The ratification of the council of Europe Istanbul convention by the EU: A step forward in the protection of women from violence in the European legal system. *European Journal of Legal Studies, 9*(2), 69–102.

Dünkel, F. (2017). European penology: The rise and fall of prison population rapes in Europe in times of migrant crises and terrorism. *European Journal of Criminology, 14*(6), 629–653.

Du Toit, L. (2007). The conditions of consent. In R. Hunter & S. Cowan (Eds.), *Choice and consent: Feminist engagements with law and subjectivity* (pp. 58–73). Routledge-Cavendish.

Edwards, A. (2010). Everyday rape: International human rights law and violence against women in peacetime. In C. McGlynn & V. E. Munro (Eds.), *Rethinking rape law: International and comparative perspectives* (pp. 92–108). Routledge.

European Union (1957, March 25). Treaty Establishing the European Community (Consolidated Version), Rome Treaty. https://www.refworld.org/docid/3ae6b39c0.html. Accessed 1 December 2021.

European Union (1997, October 2). Treaty on European Union (Consolidated Version), Treaty of Amsterdam. https://www.refworld.org/docid/3dec906d4.html. Accessed 2 December 2021.

FitzGerald, S. (2008). Putting trafficking on the map: The geography of feminist complicity. In V. E. Munro & M. Della Giusta (Eds.), *Demanding sex: Critical reflections on the regulation of prostitution* (pp. 99–120). Ashgate.

FitzGerald, S., & Freedman, J. (2021). Where is the justice in EU anti-trafficking policy? Feminist reflections on European Union policy-making processes. *European Journal of Women's Studies, 28*(4). https://doi.org/10.1177/13505068211029324

Foucault, M. (2003). *Society must be defended: Lectures at the Collège de France 1975–1976*. Penguin Books.

Foucault, M. (2009). *Security, territory, population: Lectures at the Collège de France 1977–1978*. Palgrave Macmillan.

Gill, R., & Orgad, S. (2018). The shifting terrain of sex and power: From the 'sexualization of culture' to #MeToo. *Sexualities, 21*(8), 1313–1324.

Golder, B. (2015). *Foucault and the politics of rights*. Stanford University Press.

Gruber, A. (2020). *The Feminist War on Crime: The unexpected role of women's liberation in mass incarceration*. University of California Press.

Haas, P. M. (2015). *Epistemic communities, constructivism, and international environmental politics*. Routledge.

Harris, K. L. (2019). *Beyond the rapist: Title IX and sexual violence on US campuses.* Oxford University Press.

Humbert, A. L., Strid, S., Hearn, J., & Balkmar, D. (2021). Undoing the 'Nordic Paradox': Factors affecting rates of disclosed violence against women across the EU. *PLoS one 16*(5). https://doi.org/10.e0249693

Ignjatović, S., & Bošković, A. (2013). Are we there yet? Citizens of Serbia and public policy on gender equality within the EU accession context. *European Journal of Women's Studies, 20*(4), 425–440.

Jacquot, S. (2015). *Transformations in EU gender equality: From emergence to dismantling.* Springer.

Jehle, J.-M. (2012). Attrition and conviction rates of sexual offences in Europe: Definitions and criminal justice responses. *European Journal on Criminal Policy and Research, 18*(1), 145–161.

Joachim, J. M. (2007). *Agenda setting, the UN, and NGOs: Gender violence and reproductive rights.* Georgetown University Press.

Kajta, J. (2017). Discursive strategies of polish nationalists in the construction of the other. *Intersections: East European Journal of Society and Politics, 3*(3), 88–107.

Kantola, J. (2010). *Gender and the European Union.* Macmillan International Higher Education.

Koch, M., McMillan, L., & Peper, B. (2011). Diversity, standardization and the perspective of social transformation. In M. Koch, L. McMillan, & B. Peper (Eds.), *Diversity, standardisation and social transformation: Gender, ethnicity and inequality in Europe* (pp. 213–222). Ashgate.

Kulpa, R., & Mizielińska, J. (2011). *De-centring Westerns sexualities: Central and Eastern European perspectives.* Routledge.

Kutay, A. (2014). *Governance and European civil society: Governmentality, discourse and NGOs.* Routledge.

Leahy, S. (2014). No Means No, but where's the force? Addressing the challenges of formally recognising non-violent sexual coercion as a serious criminal offence. *The Journal of Criminal Law, 78*(4), 309–325.

Liebfried, S. (2015). Social policy: Left to the judges and the markets? In H. Wallace, M. A. Pollack, & A. R. Young (Eds.), *Policy-making in the European Union.* 7th ed (pp. 263–292). Oxford University Press.

Lombardo, E., & Meier, P. (2008). Framing gender equality in the European Union political discourse. *Social Politics, 1*(1), 101–129.

Lombardo, E., & Verloo, M. (2009). Contentious citizenship: Feminist debates and practices and European challenges. *Feminist Review, 92*(1), 108–128.

MacKinnon, C. (1993). On torture: A feminist perspective on human rights. In K. Mahoney & P. Mahoney (Eds.), *Human rights in the twenty-first century: A global perspective* (pp. 21–32). Martinus Njihoff Publishers.

Marshall, J. (2009). Feminist reconstructions of universalism and the discourse of human rights. *International Journal of Law in Context*, 5(1), 87–92.

Mazey, S. (2000). Introduction: Integrating gender—Intellectual and 'real world' mainstreaming. *Journal of European Public Policy*, 7(3), 333–345.

McGlynn, C., & Munro, V. E. (2010). Rethinking rape law: An introduction. In C. McGlynn & V. E. Munro (Eds.), *Rethinking rape law: International and comparative perspectives* (pp. 1–14). Routledge.

Montoya, C. (2013). *From global to grassroots: The European Union, transnational advocacy, and combating violence against women*. Oxford University Press.

Montoya, C., & Rolandsen Agustín, L. (2013). The othering of domestic violence: The EU and cultural framings of violence against women. *Social Politics*, 20(4), 534–557.

Munro, V. E. (2010). From consent to coercion: Evaluating international and domestic frameworks for the criminalization of rape. In C. McGlynn & V. E. Munro (Eds.), *Rethinking rape law: International and comparative perspectives: Rethinking rape law: International and comparative perspectives* (pp. 17–29). Routledge.

Munro, V. E. (2017). Shifting sands? Consent, context and vulnerability in contemporary sexual offences policy in England and Wales. *Social & Legal Studies*, 26(4), 417–440.

Nevala, S. (2017). Coercive control and its impact on intimate partner violence through the lens of an EU-wide survey on violence against women. *Journal of interpersonal violence*, 32(12), 1792–1820.

Pollack, M., & Hafner-Burton, E. (2000). Mainstreaming gender in the European Union. *Journal of European public policy*, 7(3), 432–456.

Repo, J. (2016). Gender equality as biopolitical governmentality in a neoliberal European Union. *Social Politics* 23(2), 307–328.

Roggeband, C. (2021). Violence against women and gender-based violence. In G. Abels, A. Krizsán, H. MacRae, & A. van der Vleuten (Eds.), *The Routledge handbook of gender and EU politics* (pp. 352–363). Routledge.

Rose, N., & Miller, P. (1992). Political power beyond the state: Problematics of government. *The British Journal of Sociology*, 43(2), 173–205.

Rose, N., & Valverde, M. (1998). Governed by law? *Social & Legal Studies*, 7(4), 541–551.

Roseneil, S., Crowhurst, I., Hellesund, T., Santos, A. C., & Stoilova, M. (2013). Changing landscapes of heteronormativity: The regulation and normalisation of same-sex sexualities in Europe. *Social Politics*, 20(2), 165–199.

Sedef, A.-K. (2010). Contesting or affirming 'Europe'? European enlargement, aspirations for 'Europeanness' and new identities in the margins of Europe. *Journal of Contemporary European Studies, 18*(2), 181–191. https://doi.org/10.1080/14782804.2010.486971

Seibicke, H. (2020). Gender expertise in public policymaking: The European women's Lobby and the EU maternity leave directive. *Social politics: International studies in gender, state & society, 27*(2), 385–408.

Serisier, T. (2018). *Speaking out: Feminism, rape and narrative politics.* Springer.

Siegel, S. N. (2020). Rainbows and crosses: Noncompliance with EU law prohibiting sexual orientation discrimination. *Journal of European Social Policy, 30*(2), 241–258.

Smith, M., & Villa, P. (2010). The ever-declining role of gender equality in the European employment strategy. *Industrial Relations Journal, 41*(6), 526–543.

Squires, J. (2005). Is mainstreaming transformative? Theorising mainstreaming in the context of diversity and deliberation. *Social politics: International studies in gender, state & society, 12*(3), 366–388.

Stratigaki, M. (2005). Gender mainstreaming vs. positive action: An ongoing conflict in EU gender equality policy. *European Journal of Women's Studies, 12*(2), 165–186.

Stychin, C. (2003). *Governing sexuality: The changing politics of citizenship and law reform.* Hart Publishing.

Sümer, S. (2009). *European gender regimes and policies.* Ashgate.

The Swedish National Council for Crime Prevention. (2020). *Reported and cleared rapes in Europe. Difficulties of international comparisons. English version of report 2020: 2.* https://www.bra.se/bra-in-english/home/publications/archive/publications/2020-09-30-reported-and-cleared-rapes-in-europe.html. Accessed 24 July 2021.

United Nationals Declaration on the Elimination of Violence against Women. (1993). Proclaimed by General Assembly resolution 48/104 of 20 December.

van der Vleuten, A. (2007). *The price of gender equality: Member states and governance in the European Union.* Ashgate.

Vázquez, D., Aizpurua, E., Copp, J., & Ricarte, J. J. (2021). Perceptions of violence against women in Europe: Assessing individual- and country-level factors. *European Journal of Criminology, 18*(1), 566–584.

Walby, S. (2004). The European Union and gender equality: Emergent varieties of gender regime. *Social Politics, 11*(1), 4–29.

Walby, S. (2005). Gender mainstreaming: Productive tensions in theory and practice. *Social Politics: International Studies in Gender, State & Society, 12*(3), 321–343.

Walby, S., Towers, J., Balderston, S., Corradi, C., Francis, B., Heiskanen, M., Helweg-Larsen, K., Mergaert, L., Olive, P., Palmer, E., Stöckl, H., & Strid,

S. (2017). *The concept and measurement of violence against women and men.* Policy Press.

Weiner, E. (2009). Dirigism and *déjà vu* logic: The gender politics and perils of EU enlargement. *European Journal of Women's Studies, 16*(3), 211–228.

Wylie, G. (2016). *The international politics of human trafficking.* Springer.

CHAPTER 5

Forging National Sexual Politics: A Dance of Moving Targets and Sitting Ducks

Abstract This chapter describes and indicates how our four case study countries—Germany, Italy, Sweden and Poland—accept or resist EU norms and values around gender and sexuality. Focusing on prostitution and rape, it aims to offer some empirical examples of why and how prostitution and rape have become *moving targets* and *sitting ducks* between the EU and these Member States. The chapter describes how EU Member States relate to the EU's desire for ever closer union. It indicates how this creates a hierarchy of 'Europeanness' as the EU identifies some Member States as examples of 'good' Europeans for other Member States to emulate; while it represents other nations as consistently falling short of European standards in several areas. Then, it illustrates what happens when Member States resist EU harmonisation around gender and sexuality. It demonstrates how these nations' resistance to EU norms and values around gender and sexuality operate. Finally, it will address how gender and sexuality norms and values perpetuate forms of institutional racism in the context of immigration into the EU.

Keywords Case studies · Compliance · Resistance · National identity politics · 'European normative identity' · Sovereignty · Racism · Immigration

> The challenge facing the European Union is to build this new partnership between women and men, taking into account the historic and cultural diversity of the Member States, and drawing on this to develop a European approach to equality which is both pluralistic and humanistic and which constitutes the basis for action both in the Community and in the rest of the world. (Commission of the European Communities, 1996: 2)

The above quotation establishes the EU's intent around harmonisation and gender equality on two fronts. First, it identifies the role that harmonisation plays in the EU's plans for an ever closer union. And secondly, it indicates how it perceives that gender equality will advance that objective. And yet, a cursory glance at the current state of the EU's progress in both areas suggests that some challenges to realising that agenda remain. There are, of course, several reasons for this situation. In part, this is due to EU's relationship with it Member States and its governance structure. For example, on the one hand certain Member States resist implementing such policies on the grounds that it contravenes national sovereignty and nations' right to move in their best interests. On the other hand, however, the EU gives Member States' significant latitude in how they can implement these polities, even when EU Directives indicate how they should interpret and implement its recommendations (Mazey, 1998).

Up to this point in this book we have used our theoretical framework to tease out the key discourses driving European sexual politics around rape and prostitution. Now, in this chapter we want to change gears somewhat, and focus our attention on how these discourses have materiality in the on-the-ground politics shaping the discord and tension between the EU and specific Member States. Therefore, in this chapter we aim to *describe* and *indicate* rather than analyse in any great detail how our four case study countries—Germany, Italy, Sweden and Poland—accept or resist EU norms and values around gender and sexuality. As case studies these nations are interesting because they have different relationships with the EU. For example, Germany (previously West Germany) and Italy are two of the EU's founding members and Germany, in particular, is one of the 'engines' of European integration (Colegrove, 2005). Both nations have influenced how the EU has developed. For example, German policy influenced all stages of European unification, and it informed how European cohesion evolved after the end of the cold war. By contrast, Sweden joined the EU after much domestic deliberation in 1995 (Silander & Wallin, 2005). As a mid-sized European country, the international community recognises it as often 'punching above its weight' (Björkdahl, 2013). And finally, Poland joined the EU in 2004 as part of the EU expansion to the east. Its accession process was long, and Poland's ability to align with the EU's normative platform was something that both the EU and various Polish actors questioned (Maj, 2014; Szczerbiak, 2012). To join, Poland had to establish that it was able to adopt the broad sets of norms that constitute EU's *acquis communautaire* (Anderson, 2006: 106). Today, Poland's population size makes it one of the largest Member States and, therefore, a force with which the EU must reckon.

To develop our discussion in this chapter, we retain our two examples, namely prostitution and rape. In doing so, our objective is to draw the reader's attention to some empirical examples of why and how prostitution and rape have become *moving targets* and *sitting ducks* between the EU and these Member States. Discussion on this issue takes the following form. In Section One entitled: 'Learning from Thy Neighbours', we describe how EU Member States relate to the EU's desire for normative alignment via cross-Member State mutual learning and comparison. We depict how this process establishes a hierarchy of 'Europeanness' as the EU identifies some Member States as examples of 'good' Europeans for other Member States to emulate; while at the same time it represents other nations as consistently falling short of European standards in several areas. In Section Two entitled: 'Resistance to EU Normative Alignment', we illustrate what happens when Member States resist aspects of the European project around gender and sexuality. We will show how, for these nations, such resistance has become a discursive frame to propel national identity politics around anti-genderism in Poland and other Member States. In Section Three entitled: 'European and Domestic Responses to the Threat of 'the Outside' and the 'Outsider Within'', we address another way in which normative alignment around gender and sexuality has informed pan-European debates. The steep increase in arrivals of asylum seekers from Syria to Europe in 2015 challenged European values and threatened normative alignment across the Union. We will consider the discourses underpinning political debate on this issue for what it can tell us about European sexual politics.

Learning from Thy Neighbours

While critics have questioned the EU's legitimacy and sustainability in the last decade, not least due to the Euro crisis and Brexit, Europeans' scepticism about the EU is not new. We use our four cases to illustrate that this scepticism can take many different forms and come from different vantage points.

To begin, let us consider debates about the gender gap and the role they play in garnering support for EU in the 1980s and 1990s in different EU nations. In ways that illuminate why and how European institutions are gendered and perpetuate gender inequality, some EU institutions in the 1980s and 1990s have interpreted women's lack of support for the EU as a consequence of their lack of interest in and knowledge of politics (Liebert, 2013). The on-the-ground reality, however, told a different story. Because countries like Sweden, for example, where women were active in domestic politics and were, as a consequence, joining the EU as Swedish political representatives, it became clear that it was necessary to re-evaluate the appropriateness of the former analytical lens on this question. Instead of interpreting women's resistance to European harmonisation as evidence of their lack of political knowledge or their innate inability to understand politics, now it became imperative to examine whether women's reservations about EU membership were due to their well-founded and informed concerns that membership could have more negative consequences for women than men (Liebert, 2013). For example, domestic political debates in Sweden leading up to Sweden's accession to the EU in 1995 serves as an example of this situation. Among Swedish citizens generally, but especially among women, EU scepticism was due to their concern that the levels of welfare, inclusion and rights that women enjoyed in Sweden would diminish upon EU membership (Young, 2000). Gender equality is a strong norm in Sweden. It was integrated into mainstream politics long before Sweden's accession to the EU (Strid, 2020). Therefore, women had a legitimate fear that EU membership would reverse hard won feminist victories in these areas (Liebert, 2013; Young, 2000). In order to reassure its citizenry, Sweden conducted soundings of what EU accession would mean for gender equality, and it used this to make a case for joining the EU (Towns, 2002).

By contrast, women living in European countries that had not mainstreamed gender equality were more positive about the EU. This manifested in their looking to the EU to improve their status domestically, and to pressure their governments to revise national legislation to reflect its commitment to gender equality. Italy is one such example where women were more positive about the EU. Over time, women became more supportive of the EU as it enhanced its powers beyond labour and market relations (Liebert, 2013: 209). Italian women witnessed that the exemption of EU competences had a positive effect on gender equality in Italy. Thus, while it is beyond the scope of this chapter to elaborate on these dynamics, it is interesting to consider how Italian cultural and social mores around gender and sexuality inform Swedish and Italian women's view of the EU's potential to improve or disimprove their lives.

This brings us to the Polish context. While it was the case that Polish society generally supported EU membership at the time of accession, several studies show how that citizens were less supportive on this question than on other political questions (Szczerbiak, 2012). Consequently, in the period leading up to Poland's 2004 accession to the EU, gender and sexuality became increasingly politicised in Poland (Graff, 2009 in Graff & Korolczuk, 2017: 184). It would, however, be a mistake to assume that this is a new phenomenon. Successive Polish governments and some elements of the national media have, since the mid-1990s, presented gender conservatism as key to Poland's uniqueness in Europe, and as a matter of national pride linked to national sovereignty. What is interesting in the context of this chapter is that the government's attempts to meet EU thresholds to qualify for membership pushed gender equality policies in Poland in ways that tapped into wider national and cultural anxieties about 'Polishness' (Anderson, 2006; Maj, 2014).

What the above examples demonstrate is that the geopolitical history and social and cultural mores that underpin national identity politics in Member States matter. Combined these factors will colour and mediate their relationship to the EU as an idea and an institution. Therefore, we submit that for many nations EU membership is one thing, alignment with the EU's normative agendas is another thing entirely. Consequently, we glimpse significant differences between our four case study countries. At the one end of the scale, we find Sweden which embraces the EU as a normative power and seeks to enhance that function and to contribute to its priorities as an extension of domestic policy. In the process, it aims to convert other EU nations to its world view. At the other end of the scale, we find Poland, which even before its accession to the EU, expressed its reservations about how to align domestic law with EU norms. For many, these norms seemed alien to Poland.

In order to elucidate what this means for our four study countries we want to describe how, for some and in certain situations, the EU has created a window of opportunity. To be clear, we are here talking about opportunity in two different respects. First, we refer to the opportunity for Member States to transpose domestic concerns and policies around gender and sexuality into a European agenda and in the process change their meaning. And secondly, we refer to those Member States who resist EU harmonisation and norms and values around gender and sexuality and, in the process, use this 'moment' of resistance to re-enforce national identity 'at home' by re-enforcing in their vision of the nation state. In doing so, we want to demonstrate how gender and sexuality become *moving targets* and *sitting ducks* in this relational process.

Sweden is good example of a Member State that uses gender and sexuality as a *moving target* to ensure that the EU is an opportunity structure for pushing its domestic policy beyond its jurisdiction. Since its accession to the EU, Sweden has treated the EU as a platform for diffusing not only concrete policies but also a geospecific frame about the role of policy in meaning-making. As we discussed in Chapter 3, Sweden has informed how the EU has approached the issues of prostitution. It did so by redefining it as an gender equality issue. Outshoorn et al. describe how Swedish feminist civil society actors and politicians were able to instrumentalise the possibilities that arose in the 1990s with the fall of the Berlin Wall. They argue that the ensuing 'ideological void' became a 'major organising principle' because 'it opened the ways for a third wave of feminist mobilisation' (2012: 133).

Armed with the experience garnered through decades of political activity, Sweden's EU representatives have, since its accession, taken an active role in promoting gender equality through their contributions to various EU bodies. In Swedish debates leading up to EU membership and also due to the publication of a 1993 governmental report, proponents of EU membership argued that a point in favour of Sweden joining the EU was that it provided a vehicle for Sweden to share its expertise internationally (Towns, 2002). An example on the pulse of this national self-belief in Sweden's is how it has embraced the role of norm entrepreneur. For example, prior to taking on the presidency of the Council of Europe and a few years after Swedish accession, the Swedish government prepared to 'exhibit Swedish culture in Europe' in which they counted gender equality as one of Sweden's unique accomplishments (Towns, 2002: 157).

Elsewhere, and in ways that diametrically oppose the Swedish approach, Italian civil society actors have used the EU as a *sitting duck* or a lever for pushing agendas at home. Italy was hit hard by the economic recession of 2008 and, similar to other countries, this worsened conditions for women socially, politically and economically. This occurred against a backdrop where right-wing political agendas began to retrieve 'traditional' discourses around gender and sexuality which they promoted as more Italian (Chironi, 2020). This resistance to EU norms on gender equality notwithstanding, EU membership and the effect of Europeanisation in Italy (Fabbrini & Piattoni, 2008; Franchino & Radaelli, 2004) has influenced the uptake in Italian hard law and soft law policies around gender equality and VAW (Donà, 2012: 102). This is evident also in how Italian citizens generally, and civil society actors specifically, see the EU's potential to improve the domestic situation. Support for the EU builds also on its potential to prevent successive Italian governments from retreating from their commitments to gender equality and LGTBQI rights as EU Member States (Chironi, 2020; Montoya, 2013). This interaction between civil society actors on local, national and EU levels produces what is sometimes referred to in the literature as 'a boomerang effect' (Keck & Sikkink, 1998 cited in Walby, 2004: 16). Simply put: for civil society pressure to work, then the national government must care about any negative consequences that will follow if they do not act. On this issue Montoya claims that: 'Normative strategies are effective when states are open to persuasion and accept the promoted norms' (2013: 34). In this way, the EU provides civil society actors with an alternative political space from which to mobilise beyond the nation state. In such circumstances, the possibility for change emerges when governments and politicians alike fear the negative, external attention to national politics. It is this that will compel them to change tack. An example of this occurred in 2012 when a coalition of 12 Italian feminist organisations mobilised at the domestic and international level under the heading 'No More' (violence), demanding that the Italian government ratify the Istanbul Convention. They argued that a coordinated legislative action against VAW and the strategic use of international normative standards for promoting such action to address VAW in Italy would enable them to overcome what they perceived as the 'deliberate policy of inactivity chosen by the government' (Donà, 2018: 235).

Viewed in this way, it is clear that in both practical and normative terms, Member States have an important role to play in serving as either role models for 'best practice' or examples of what not to do. As the EU regulates gender and sexuality via soft law policies, normative alignment across Member States serves a particularly important function. As Vukasović observes:

> The EU is discursively constructed as a value community where commitment to shared, "core", liberal values steer the activities of its members and at the same time serve as a "role model" that encourages others to adopt the same values. (2020: 61)

Thus, while there are many factors that determine Member States' position on the hierarchy of 'Europeanness', adhering to the correct European values is both a requirement for community membership, something that when it is lacking means that Member States risk being negatively compared to others and subsequently shamed into alignment.

Ever since Sweden joined the EU in 1995, it has consistently ranked first on various gender equality rankings, including the European Institute for Gender Equality (EIGE) index which, in 2020, placed Sweden as the most gender equal country of the EU, a ranking based on the situation across societal domains.[1] It should be noted here, however, that feminists have been critical of the EIGE, arguing that its governance structures are the same as other EU institutions. This means that it is a technocratic tool of the EU that provides it with statistical rather than granular data about the 'on-the-ground-reality' of gender equality in individual contexts (Hubert & Stratigaki, 2011). Perhaps it is due to this lacuna that it presents Sweden as a gender equality role model within the EU. We find evidence of this in the Report *Exploring Best Practices in Combatting Violence Against Women: Sweden* (Policy Department for Citizens' Rights and Constitutional Affairs, 2018: 8). The Report states that: 'The Scandinavian nation is a forerunner of gender equality driven by both an intellectual and practical feminist movement'. Meanwhile, Germany debated the applicability of 'best practice' established by other

---

[1] Available at: https://eige.europa.eu/publications/gender-equality-index-2020-sweden. Accessed 20 June 2021.

European countries, especially Sweden (Maj, 2014). While gender experts interviewed by Maj were looking to Scandinavia for inspiration, they were more ambivalent about the EU's attempts to use Scadinavian countries, including Sweden, as an example of the 'best practice' approach (Maj, 2014).

As mentioned in Chapter 3, Sweden's accession to the EU is said to have pushed the EU's gender agenda in a specific direction. It is important to note, however, that this influence took another route and not in the way envisaged by the EU. As we discussed above, in Swedish debates about joining the EU, fears over how membership would worsen Swedish society were evident. It is in this context that the issue of prostitution surfaced. Feminists and politicians argued that in order to protect Sweden from the negative effects of policy creep from Brussels and elsewhere, the government had to initiate legislative reform on sex purchase (Gould, 2001). As the campaign gained momentum, campaigners linked this marginal issue to the perceived lack of gender equality in the EU and EU Member States, as Sweden saw it (and indeed it does still) (Strid, 2020). In this way, campaigners used prostitution as a *moving target* to feed a particular kind of national identity politics that promoted the view that Sweden was more advanced than other nations in terms of its policies on gender (Liebert, 2013; Strid, 2020).

Similarly, Sweden has emerged as 'the leader of the pack' in terms of gender equality policies and as 'among the European countries with the most proactive policies on violence against women' (Hearn et al., 2016: 556; see also Maj, 2014). In Chapter 3, we described the road to the 2014 European Parliament (EP) Resolution that proposed that all EU Member States should criminalise the purchase of sex and decriminalise the sale of sex. In short, the EP adopted a Swedish policy as EU policy uncritically. This result reveals something about how the EU operates by identifying certain nations as examples of 'best practice' for other countries to emulate. And yet, this does not take fully into consideration the discrepancies in standards across the EU, and what might merit the label 'best practice' in one context, will not necessarily work well in another for several important reasons (Crowhurst & Skilbrei, 2018). What we described in Chapter 3 as the pull of 'the Swedish model' of prostitution policy is part of this trend across the Union. This is why, for example, we see that prostitution law and policy debates in countries that are very different from Sweden, such as Ireland, discuss policy transfer as a 'quick fix' to perceived national problems around gender equality and human trafficking (FitzGerald & McGarry, 2016). We find similar issues in Italian politics where government and civil society actors promote the benefits of the 'Swedish model' without due attention to the practical aspects of what applying this geospecific piece of legislation might mean in a radically different socio-economic and cultural context (Crowhurst, 2017).

As the EU has moved more into gender and sexuality law and policies, the elements involved in what produces the hierarchy between Member States shifts. Size and economic muscle may constitute a 'good' EU Member State. But today, individual nations' ability to provide evidence of their normative alignment with EU norms and values is becoming even more important. This means that Member States who are exemplars of 'good' practice may be able to avoid negative comparison in other policy areas. As mentioned in Chapter 4, there are currently discussions afoot within the EU to amend rape legislation to better align it with contemporary ideas about sexuality and new views on what supports sexual integrity. Such debates have also been going on in Sweden. In 2018, it changed its rape law to criminalise the presence of non-voluntariness rather than violence or force. While the process leading up to the 2018 legislative revision was long, and lawmakers assessed possible solutions at length, the argument that Sweden needed to change its rape laws in order to meet its international obligations, such as the Istanbul Convention, was almost non-existent. Instead, debates revolved around a discourse that represented the revision process as uniquely Swedish, even though the definition of rape as a sexual act taking place without consent was already in existence in many jurisdictions, including major European ones (see Nilsson, 2019). Reading these debates it is striking that they do not touch upon the need for Sweden to consider normative alignment with other countries and to draw on other nations' experiences with such legislation (Skilbrei, 2021).

At this point in our discussion it is useful to return to the Polish context. While the pressure from the EU during the accession process meant that the Polish government needed to implement several gender equality instruments at once. The reality is that joining the EU has not furthered its gender equality agenda much (Maj, 2014). In fact, recent political moves demonstrate that Poland continues to adopt regressive measures in this area. As the EU supports the involvement of networked expertise on gender equality, it is itself becoming a force to be reckoned with in the policy sphere. And yet, the lack of such networks *in* Poland (Maj, 2014) means that the interplay between policy development and legitimisation functions differently in Poland than in many other Member States and, as a consequence, this means that it is often at odds with the EU. Mobilisation around gender equality more broadly, and prostitution and rape more specifically, is not strong in Poland (Anderson, 2006; Maj, 2014). In a context where the government has been consistently rolling back hard won rights and protections for women and the LGBTQI community, it has been difficult for Polish women's organisations, for example, to sustain a strong and consolidated political movement domestically, and indeed to secure the governmental support necessary to push and protect gender equality policies for all (Maj, 2014).

This means that the EU defines Poland geopolitically as 'Eastern European' and this translates often into it being counted as 'Europe but not Europe' (Wolff, 1994 in Mälksoo, 2006: 276). Gender and sexual norms identify a long fault line between East and West in Europe. During the Soviet era, women's exclusion from the political sphere was part of a phenomenon that some commentators have referred to as 'Central European illiberalism'. Key for our purposes is that this is a political context in which these nations juxtapose their worldview with what it perceives as the encroachment and threatening imperialism of 'Europeaness' (Ramme, 2019).

In the following section, we ask that the reader keep this in mind as we explore in more detail the trajectory of Poland's accession to the EU and its conflicts with and resistance to EU normative alignment within the Union around gender and sexuality.

Resistance to EU Normative Alignment

The Treaty of Lisbon (TFEU 2007) identifies gender equality as a matter of law for all EU Member States. And yet, as we have seen, not all countries agree that they should be subject to the Treaty and its obligations. Poland is one of the two EU countries that has assumed a derogation from the Treaty, in what is often referred to as the 'British Protocol' (Maj, 2014: 13). Poland represents its refusal to adopt the Treaty and the subsequent ramifications for the Charter for Fundamental Rights, as an infringement on its right to legislate on matters to do with 'public morality, family law, the protection of human dignity and moral and physical integrity' (Maj, 2014: 13). In this way, gender and sexuality have become a *moving target* around the meaning of morality, dignity relative to the Polish body politic and a *sitting duck* in discussions around the need for Poland to resist the transposition of EU gender equality policies (Anderson, 2006).

It is worthwhile taking a closer look at the kind of resistance to the normative alignment across the EU, for which Poland has become notorious. Poland has received considerable EU level criticism for its failure to implement anti-discrimination measures. In its 2014 Report on Poland, the Committee on the Elimination of Discrimination against Women (CEDAW), raised concerns about the lack of a general prohibition against unequal treatment of men and women in Polish law.[2] The EU found that Poland's efforts to harmonise gender equality policies left much to be desired in the accession process (Anderson, 2006). At that time, the Catholic Church and aligned civil society actors voiced their resistance to harmonisation of gender equality norms before the accession negotiations, and found support among right wing political parties (Anderson, 2006). In interviews with Polish experts, Maj (2014) found that many believed that joining the EU did not mean that Poland had to adhere to higher standards in terms of gender equality, but rather they believed that Poland could use its position in the EU to reduce said standards. Still, Maj sums up: 'The EU has provided Poles with the language of gender equality, fulfilling a gap in the terminology and popularizing the use of a number of concepts' (2014: 144).

While part of Poland's socialist heritance is a high level of women's participation in the labour market (Maj, 2014), equal opportunities were not a formal principle in Poland until its accession to the EU (Anderson, 2006). In the years preceding EU membership, Poland has witnessed several unsuccessful attempts to introduce domestic gender equality legislation (Anderson, 2006). Since 1989, an anti-feminist rhetoric that originated in specific men's groups' activism and discourse has dominated Polish public discourses. Combined, these groups have aided right wing political efforts to bring this rhetoric into the mainstream political imaginary (Wojnicka, 2016). This follows from a general rejection of feminism which, in these quarters, is considered a Western ideology. It is important to note, however, that women are not absent from this framing-exercise. Since the fall of the Soviet Bloc, local women's movements occupied post-communist space and rejected

---

[2] Available at: https://tbinternet.ohchr.org/_layouts/15/treatybodyexternal/Download.aspx?symbolno=CEDAW/C/POL/CO/7-8&Lang=En. Accessed 20 June 2021.

the idea that asking the state to intervene more in family life and private space was a good idea for them (Sharp, 1996: 102). On the one hand, this retreat from state intervention in family and private life is understandable in light of women's experiences under socialism. On the other hand, however, this stance has had some unintended consequences for gender equality in Poland. In short, it has produced a situation in which the media, the medical and governmental institutions as arms of the state, use gender equality as a *moving target* to promote radicalised models of masculinity and femininity that invoke traditional and conservative meanings of male and female gender roles, consistent with what Connell and Messerschmidt (2005) term hegemonic masculinity and subordinated femininity.

Anderson (2006) makes the point that it is necessary to see the relationship between EU and the national level not as an interaction between two already existing positions, but as something that forms opportunities and actions more thoroughly. Her example is how in relation to the Polish EU accession (Anderson, 2006: 107): 'The financial and political resources of the European Union reshape the domestic political landscape in these countries by providing incentives for groups to promote gender equity policies that are in line with EU directives'. This is a more positive take on the relationship between Poland and the EU than offered by Maj (2014), and also on the progress made in gender equality.

This brings us to Poland's stance on VAW. In 2012, Poland, along with other European countries, signed the Istanbul Convention. At that time, the Polish Parliament indicated that it planned to move forward towards ratification. And yet, when the government attempted to transpose the Istanbul Convention into Polish law this prompted strong backlash from parliamentary members and civil society groups, including feminist NGOs and victims' organisations on the one hand, and Catholic and conservative NGOs and masculinist groups, such as the *Masculinum Foundation* and fathers' rights organisations, on the other. In this political space, such organisations felt pushed into 'emergency mode' to respond to the perceived threat that the Convention and 'European values' posed to the nation and the survival of 'Polishness' (Grzebalska & Pető, 2018). In this way, rape and VAW became a *moving target* around meaning of 'Polishness' as public debates demonised 'foreign' gender equality politics. In a statement by the Polish President, Andrzej Duda, the Istanbul Convention represented an infringement of 'European values that were oppositional to our traditional values'. In the minds of opponents, this threat established the need for a 'common sense' approach to what was 'appropriate', 'normal' and 'legitimate' in Poland around sexual politics (Ramme, 2019).

For around three years, a significant number of Polish parliamentarians argued that Poland could not ratify the Convention because it was contrary not only to *Polish values* but also to the *Polish Constitution*. Primarily, opponents pointed to Article 19 of the Constitution on the protection of family, motherhood, marriage and children, arguing that the Convention contravenes the Constitution by imposing on the state the obligation to tackle gender stereotypes and cultural practices that discriminate against women (Warat, 2014). Invoking a nationalist-religious discourse that identified the meaning of gender equality as a 'civilisation of death', 'genderism' and 'dżender' (gender), opponents began an anti-gender campaign.

Król and Pustulka (2018) argue that it was protests around abortion that prompted the government to consider revoking the Istanbul Convention. Furthermore, at this time it ceased funding the largest Polish NGO, the Centre for Women's Rights and Blue Line, an organisation which focused on gender-based violence. In doing so, it hoped to halt what it defined as feminist and homo-propaganda.

During the summer of 2013, Bishop Tadeusz Peronnek stated from the pulpit, 'I would like to add that gender ideology is worse than communism and nazism put together'. Graff (2014) claims that this framing indicates a step change in political strategies in Poland. Officially inaugurated by the Bishops' Conference of Poland in a pastoral letter, which was read in most parishes on 29 December 2013, this pastoral letter consolidated the religious right by declaring war on 'gender ideology'. Among other things the letter claimed:

> [G]ender ideology is the product of many decades of ideological and cultural changes that are deeply rooted in Marxism and neo-Marxism, endorsed by some feminist movements and the sexual revolution. ... According to this ideology, humans can freely determine whether they want to be men or women and freely choose their sexual orientation. ... We call on educational institutions to engage in the promotion of an integral vision of man.'[3]

---

[3] Full text in English translation can be found at https://rorate-caeli.blogspot.com/2014/02/bishops-attack-dangerous-gender.html. Accessed 20 June 2021.

As part of its political campaign, the Conference created posters warning against 'genderism' and the 'sexualisation of children' in schools throughout the country. Furthermore, 'concerned parents' sent petitions to local officials demanding bans on sex education. Teachers, who were rumoured to discuss gender in the classroom, experienced harassment or were dismissed.

In a move that demonstrates the strength of opposition to the Istanbul Convention and how it became a *sitting duck* in Poland, in January 2014, the Polish Parliament established a so-called *Anti-gender Ideology Parliamentary Committee*. Its official goals are:

> [To] defend the sex identity of a human being and work towards the establishment of legislation changes which will protect *traditional families* [emphasis in original] and support pro-family politics ... develop solutions regarding possibilities of combating the negative influence of gender ideology on children's education.[4]

Taken together, the level of controversy raised by the Convention among the Catholic Church hierarchy and political establishment indicated significant opposition to women's rights (Wojnicka, 2016). In a context where Polish national identity politics are rooted in Polands geopolitical connections to the former Soviet Union, gender and the notion of 'gender ideology' as 'foreign' threats to the nation function as the symbolic glue and as a strawman that emboldens far-right groups and organisations. Specifically, it emboldens them to unite and mobilise around the umbrella of 'cultural hegemony' and 'common sense' values that preserve Polishness from external encroachment (Laclau & Mouffe, 1985).

What we witness in the Polish response to the Istanbul Convention is not unique. It is happening across the EU. We argue that Poland's response is not only an expression of local unrest and social tension, But rather we submit that it must be understood as another expression of the transnational social movement against the EU (Korolczuk & Graff, 2018). This means that it is not sufficient to analyse this anti-gender movement as stemming from Catholicism or particular gender regimes alone as anti-genderism crosses religious and political divides (ibid.).

---

[4] Available at: https://www.sejm.gov.pl/sejm7.nsf/agent.xsp?symbol=ZESPOL&Zesp=276. Accessed 20 June 2021.

We find evidence of similar 'anti-gender' demonstrations in Italy. In terms that perhaps resonate with Italy's constant struggle with corruption at all levels of society, opposition to gender takes the form of resistance to the alleged corruption of gender and sexuality norms in society (Paternotte & Kuhar, 2017). In this way, gender equality takes on particular meaning and as a result it becomes a *moving target*. An important backdrop to anti-genderism in Italy is the role of familialism, which is rooted in how the Catholic Church emphasises the sanctity of the family (Garbagnoli, 2017: 166). Of course, it is the case that anti-gender sentiments exist in secular countries such as Sweden too. There, they operate within the populist right-wing nationalist party, the Swedish Democrats. For them, gender equality stems from so-called international elites or from a 'neo colonial' EU (Paternotte & Kuhar, 2017). When we argue that expressions of anti-genderism can be found throughout Europe, it is to demonstrate the larger backdrop of Member States' responses to the EU's attempts to move into more normative territory. While not all of these protests are directed at the EU or indeed for the same reasons. What unites them is that they occur in opposition to 'outsiders', and what these nations perceive as EU attempts to override national norms. In Section Two entitled: 'European and Domestic Responses to the Threat of 'the Outside' and the 'Outsider Within'', we turn our attention to how normative alignment around gender and sexuality is related to pan-European debates about migration.

European and Domestic Responses to the Threat of 'the Outside' and the 'Outsider Within'

While controversies over the EU's normative agenda continue to soar in Poland, German sexual politics take a different form. In this context, they do not revolve around the perceived need to a push against law and policy coming from outside the nation state, but rather how 'outsiders within' i threaten Germany's functioning as a liberal society and, as a consequence destabilise German gender and sexuality norms and values. To understand what has formed the contemporary German situation, we take as an entry point for analysis events that transpired in Köln on New Year's Eve 2015. These events triggered deep-seated anxieties in Germany about the link between migration, Islam, sexuality and modern-day 'German identity' which surged in the media and in political fora for months to come.

As civil war in Syria and the wider Middle East proliferated since 2011, eventually this prompted the mass exodus of refugees out of the region during the summer months of 2015. Initially Germany, conscious of its history of intolerance around issues of race, identity and belonging and in response to protests from far-right anti refugee organisations like Pegida (Patriotic Europeans against the Islamisation of the West), attempted to demonstrate German *Willkommenskultur* by accepting over one million refugees. The words of then German Kanzlerin, Dr. Angela Merkel, became emblematic of a 'moment' in the maturation of the German identity when she offered the words that defined public debate 'at home' and overseas that long, hot summer. She stated: '*Wir haben so vieles geschafft – wir schaffen das*' (We have coped with so much—We can cope with this).[5] In short, this 'moment' became a *moving target* around the meaning of modern German identity in the face of its troubled history.

Quickly, however, this sentiment came under attack from various quarters and it became a *sitting duck* in wider German politics around immigration. During the first few days of 2016 and just weeks after the Chancellery approved a new federal law on sexual assault, the German media released reports of a series of sexual assaults on New Year's Eve at Köln's main train station. The first reports appeared in a local newspaper, the *Kölner Stadt-Anzeiger* and on the Pegida Facebook page. Soon, other media began to engage with the story. On the 9th and 10th of January 2016, two German newspapers released two images that tapped into deep-seated fears over the Muslim 'other' posing a threat to German values.

Weber (2019) observed that the media coverage invoked gendered and sexualised discourses of racial difference that in Germany was generally taboo. She suggests that this marks the moment when German public discourse pivots towards a radical right-wing frame based on the perceived rather than the real threats to German national identity and the nation. Consequently, in the days and weeks that followed, the German and international media became consumed with discussion about the dangers of 'political correctness', Germany's 'too liberal' immigration policies and, once again, 'Muslim patriarchy' in Germany and throughout the EU (Boulila & Carri, 2017).

---

[5] https://www.politico.eu/article/the-phrase-that-haunts-angela-merkel/. Accessed 24 April 2021.

A superficial examination of the media reports at this time reveals how certain members of the German political class and the mainstream media use the sexual assaults against German women (read white) in Köln as a proxy to retrieve the longstanding legal debate about the need to set boundaries around 'German identity' and 'German values'. When the German Parliament resumed after the Christmas break, representatives from across the political spectrum debated the importance of police protection of public safety and especially for (German white) women. The responses to these events is reminiscent of how historically, women's sexual integrity comes to stand for the integrity of the nation (Outshoorn et al., 2012). Commentators note that this is not surprising:

> [B]ecause nationalism, gender and sexuality are all socially and culturally constructed, they frequently play an important role in constructing one another – by invoking and helping to construct the "us" versus "them" distinction and the exclusion of the Other. The empowerment of one gender, one nation or one sexuality virtually always occurs at the expense and disempowerment of another. (Mayer, 2000: 1)

In recent years, the literature has termed how nationalist agendas throughout Europe have harnessed the 'protection' of women and instrumentalised feminist agendas as 'femonationalism' (Farris, 2017). Farris intended the term to cover a much broader phenomenon than far-right extremisms' co-option of women's rights when she described also how 'femocrats' act and invoked femonationalist tactics when representing western gender norms as superior and the woman of the Muslim 'other' as inherently oppressed. Furthermore, after decades of political indifference to sexual violence, suddenly the German Parliament was consumed by the need to reform Germany's rape law.[6] As post-Köln debates dismissed charges of racism as 'hysteria', the event triggered the amendment of German rape law and hastened Germany's adoption of the Istanbul Convention.

---

[6] The CDU Party had, up to that point, been resistant to changing the definition of rape. Previously, rape law in Germany stipulated that sexual crimes could not be prosecuted as sexual assault or rape unless the victim could demonstrate physical resistance to the attack.

In ways that make the case that sexual violence can be both a *moving target* and a *sitting duck* and often simultaneously, in order to uphold the post-feminist contention that sexual violence can only be a result of 'open borders', the German Parliament linked the criminal law governing sexual violence to the need to revise the German Residence Act (2008) 'to manage the influx of foreigners into the Federal Republic of Germany'. The revised Act came into force in 2017.[7] In this way, it furthered a punitive gendered and racialised agenda both via criminal law and immigration law. Importantly, instead of addressing the inadequate laws governing sexual violence among the German population, the Parliamentary debate continued to focus on expelling those radicalised and gendered 'Others' who were believed to endanger post-feminist Germany (Boulila & Carri, 2017). Key here, is that Germany's response to sexual violence is that it framed it as a problem that comes from outside of Europe. According to this narrative, this is violence that is inherent to 'Other' cultures and not German or other western cultures.

Germany is not the only EU Member State where the question of gender equality becomes attached to a racialised figuring of the nation. Gender equality is key to Swedish national identity (Giritli Nygren et al., 2018) to the point that Sweden has declared itself the home of the world's first feminism government.[8] There is, though, both domestic and international critique of both the reality of Sweden as a gender equality haven, and the way Sweden promotes itself as such. From within Sweden, there is powerful critique that this constitutes a gender equality myth (Alm et al., 2021; Martinsson et al., 2017), and that this contributes to perpetuating racialised myths that construe 'the outside' and 'outsiders' as threatening to the nation and to its women (Sager & Mulinari, 2018). Sweden presents gender equality not only as something at which Sweden is better than other countries, but it is also used as a dividing line domestically as Muslim migrants are presented as lacking in gender equality (Towns, 2002). In this way, gender equality becomes a *moving target* used to define 'Swedishness' and a *sitting duck* or proxy to re-enforce the boundaries of that discrete identity.

---

[7] Available at: https://www.gesetze-im-internet.de/englisch_aufenthg/englisch_aufenthg.html#p0023. Accessed 3 October 2021.

[8] Available at: https://www.regeringen.se/informationsmaterial/2019/03/en-feministisk-regering/. Accessed 1 July 2020.

Conclusion: Is an Ever Closer Union on Track in the EU?

The fact that different EU Member States draw a line between individual and collective interests and between public concerns and privacy differently, has consequences for how they relate to policies forged on an EU level. Maj (2014: 279) indicates that what causes a controversy in Member States' relationship with the EU vary. For example, in the case of Poland, topics related to reproductive law and relationships between people of the same sex raise concerns. While in Germany, conflicts emerges around anti-discrimination, the individual's freedom to act in their own interests, gender equality in the private sector, the strategy of gender mainstreaming and the institutional care for children.

Conflicts over gender issues and sexuality are salient (Rubin, 1984), and this is something that we have tried to demonstrate throughout this book. What is at stake is not only membership of particular nations in the EU and the European normative community, but also the sexual citizenship of the peoples of Europe. When the Prime Minister of Hungary, Viktor Orbán, and others declare categorically that the EU is or acts as a colonial organisation, then this is a strategic but also a loaded response to how the EU has become more involved in its Member States' domestic affairs. Current attempts to nationalise gender and sexuality norms means that they are treated as both *moving targets* and *sitting ducks*, rendering them as a resource to be used by right wing actors to delegitimise feminism and to strengthen what they see as the integrity of the nation, the family and the Church. At the same time, it is necessary to think critically about what and how gender and sexuality norms are harmonised across the Union. The sexual politics of Europe disciplines prospective and current Member States, thus making gender and sexuality part of how the EU establishes 'Europeanness as a civilizational space' (Dzenovska, 2018: 3).

References

Alm, E., Berg, L., Hero, M. L., Johansson, A., Laskar, P., Martinsson, L., Mulinari, D., & Wasshede, C. (2021). Introduction. In E. Alm, L. Berg, M. L. Hero, A. Johansson, P. Laskar, L. Martinsson, D. Mulinari, & C. Wasshede (Eds.), *Pluralistic struggles in gender, sexuality and coloniality* (pp. 1–18). Palgrave Macmillan.

Anderson, L. S. (2006). European Union gender regulations in the East: The Czech and Polish accession process. *East European Politics and Societies, 20*(1), 101–125.

Björkdahl, A. (2013). Ideas and norms in Swedish peace policy. *Swiss Political Science Review, 19*(3), 322–337.

Boulila, S. C., & Carri, C. (2017). On Cologne: *Gender*, migration and unacknowledged racisms in Germany. *European Journal of Women's Studies, 24*(3), 286–293.

Chironi, D. (2020). A fragile shield for protecting civil rights: The European Union in the eyes of Italian feminists. *European Journal of Cultural and Political Sociology, 7*(3), 316–346.

Colegrove, D. F. W. (2005). Steadfastly European? German (supra)national identity in a rapidly changing Europe. In R. Robyn (Ed.), *The changing face of European identity* (pp. 115–139). Routledge.

Commission of the European Communities. (1996). Communication from the commission: Incorporating equal opportunities for women and men into all community policies and activities, COM(96)67 final of 21 February 1996.

Connell, R., & Messerschmidt, J. (2005). Hegemonic masculinity: Rethinking the concept. *Gender & Society, 19*(6), 829–859.

Crowhurst, I. (2017). Troubling unknowns and certainties in prostitution policy claims-making. In M. Spanger & M.-L. Skilbrei (Eds.), *Prostitution research in context: Methodology, representation and power* (pp. 47–64). Routledge.

Crowhurst, I., & Skilbrei, M.-L. (2018). International comparative explorations of prostitution policies: Lessons from two European projects. *Innovation: The European Journal of Social Science Research, 3*(2), 142–161.

Donà, A. (2012). Using the EU to promote gender equality policy in traditional context: Reconciliation of work and family life in Italy. In E. Lombardo & M. Forest (Eds.), *The Europeanisation of gender equality policies: A discursive-sociological approach* (pp. 99–120). Palgrave Macmillan.

Donà, A. (2018). How do international norms matter? The impact of the Convention on the Elimination of all Forms of Discrimination Against Women in Italy. *Italian Political Science Review, 48*(2), 221–241.

Dzenovska, D. (2018). *School of Europeanness: Tolerance and other lessons in political liberalism in Latvia*. Cornell University Press.

Fabbrini, S., & Piattoni, S. (2008). *Italy in the European Union: Redefining national interest in a compound polity*. Rowman & Littlefield.

Farris, S. R. (2017). *In the name of women's rights: The rise of femonationalism*. Duke University Press.

FitzGerald, S., & McGarry, K. (2016). Problematizing prostitution in law and policy in the Republic of Ireland: A case for reframing. *Social & Legal Studies, 25*(3), 289–309.

Franchino, F., & Radaelli, C. M. (2004). Europeanisation and the Italian political system: Politics and policy. *Journal of European Public Policy, 11*(6), 941–953.

Garbagnoli, S. (2017). Italy as a lighthouse: Anti-gender protests between the "anthropological question" and national identity. In D. Paternotte & R. Kuhar (Eds.), *Anti-gender campaigns in Europe: Mobilizing against equality* (pp. 151–173). Rowman & Littlefield.

Giritli Nygren, K., Martinsson, L., & Mulinari, D. (2018). Gender equality and beyond: At the crossroads of neoliberalism, anti-gender movements, "European" values, and normative reiterations in the Nordic model. *Social Inclusion, 6*(4), 1–7.

Gould, A. (2001). The criminalisation of buying sex: The politics of prostitution in Sweden. *Journal of Social Policy, 30*(3), 437–456.

Graff, A. (2014). Report from the gender trenches: War against 'genderism' in Poland. *European Journal of Women's Studies, 21*(4), 431–435.

Graff, A., & Korolczuk, E. (2017). "Worse than communism and Nazism put together": War on gender in Poland. In D. Paternotte & R. Kuhar (Eds.), *Anti-gender campaigns in Europe: Mobilizing against equality* (pp. 175–193). Rowman & Littlefield.

Grzebalska, W., & Pető, A. (2018). The gendered modus operandi of the illiberal transformation in Hungary and Poland. *Women Studies International Forum, 68*, 164–172.

Hearn, J., Strid, S., Husu, L., & Verloo, M. (2016). Interrogating violence against women and state violence policy: Gendered intersectionalities and the quality of policy in the Netherlands, Sweden, and the UK. *Current Sociology, 64*(4), 551–567.

Hubert, A., & Stratigaki, M. (2011). The European institute of gender equality: A window of opportunity for gender equality policies? *European Journal of Women's Studies, 8*(2), 169–181.

Korolczuk, E., & Graff, A. (2018). Gender as 'Ebola from Brussels': The anti-colonial frame and the rise of illiberal populism. *Journal of Women in Culture and Society, 43*(4), 797–821. https://doi.org/10.1086/696691

Król, A., & Pustulka, P. (2018). Women on strike: Mobilizing against reproductive injustice in Poland. *International Feminist Journal of Politics, 20*(3), 366–384.

Laclau, E., & Mouffe, C. (1985). *Hegemony and socialist strategy: Towards a radical democratic politics.* Verso.

Liebert, U. (2013). Gender politics in the European Union: The return of the public. *European Societies, 1*(2), 197–239.

Maj, J. (2014). *Gender equality in the European Union: A comparative Study of Poland and Germany.* Nomos.

Martinsson, L., Griffin, G., & Giritli Nygren, K. (2017). Introduction: Challenging the myth of gender equality in Sweden. In L. Martinsson, G.

Griffin & K. Giritli Nygren (Eds.), *Challenging the myth of gender equality in Sweden* (pp. 1–22). Polity Press.

Mayer, T. (2000). Gender ironies of nationalism: Setting the stage. In T. Mayer (Ed.), *Gender ironies of nationalism: Sexing the nation* (pp. 1–22). Routledge.

Mazey, S. (1998). The European Union and women's rights: From the Europeanization of national agendas to the nationalization of a European agenda? *Journal of European Public Policy, 5*(1), 131–152.

Montoya, C. (2013). *From global to grassroots: The European Union, transnational advocacy, and combating violence against women.* Oxford University Press.

Mälksoo, M. (2006). From existential politics towards normal politics? The Baltic states in the enlarged Europe. *Security Dialogue, 37*(3), 275–329.

Nilsson, G. (2019). Towards voluntariness in Swedish rape law: Hyper-medialised group rape cases and the shift in legal discourse. In M. Heinskou, M.-L. Skilbrei, & K. Stefansen (Eds.), *Rape in the Nordic countries: Continuities and change* (pp. 101–119). Routledge.

Outshoorn, J., Kulawik, T., Dudová, R., & Prata, A. (2012). Remaking bodily citizenship in multicultural Europe: The struggle for autonomy and self-determination. In B. Halsaa, S. Roseneil, & S. Sümer (Eds.), *Remaking citizenship in multicultural Europe: Women's movements, gender and diversity* (pp. 118–140). Palgrave Macmillan.

Paternotte, D., & Kuhar, R. (2017). "Gender Ideology" in movement: Introduction. In R. Kuhar & D. Paternotte (Eds.), *Anti-gender campaigns in Europe: Mobilising against equality* (pp. 1–22). Rowman & Littlefield.

Policy Department for Citizens' Rights and Constitutional Affairs. (2018). *Exploring best practices in combatting violence against women: Sweden.* Available: https://www.europarl.europa.eu/RegData/etudes/IDAN/2018/604958/IPOL_IDA(2018)604958_EN.pdf. Accessed 24 Apr 2021.

Ramme, J. (2019). Exclusion through inclusion. Struggles over the scalar regimes of belonging *Europe* and the *Family* at the 1995 Fourth UN World Conference on Women and the Agency of *(Polish) Women. Frontiers in Sociology, 4*(55). https://doi.org/10.3389/fsoc.2019.00055

Rubin, G. (1984). Thinking sex: Notes for a radical theory of the politics of sexuality. In C. Vance (Ed.), *Pleasure and danger: Exploring female sexuality* (pp. 267–319). Routledge.

Sager, M., & Mulinari, D. (2018, May–June). Safety for whom? Exploring femonationalism and care-racism in Sweden. *Women's Studies International Forum, 68*, 149–156.

Sharp, J. (1996). Gendering nationhood: A feminism engagement with national identity. In N. Duncan (Ed.), *Bodyspace* (pp. 97–108). Routledge.

Silander, D., & Wallin, C. (2005). Being a Swede in a transforming European setting: The structures of an emerging Swedish supranational identity in the twenty-first century. In R. Robyn (Ed.), *The changing face of European identity* (pp. 207–223). Routledge.

Skilbrei, M.-L. (2021). Keeping Sweden on top: Rape and legal innovation as nation-branding. In E. Larsen, S. Moss, & I. Skjelsbæk (Eds.), *Gender equality and nation branding in the Nordic region* (pp. 75–89). Routledge.

Strid, S. (2020). Gender equality policy: From equal treatment to intersectional gender equality. In D. Silander & M. Öhlén (Eds.), *Sweden and the European Union: An assessment of the influence of EU-membership on eleven policy areas in Sweden* (pp. 159–182). Santérus Academic Press Sweden.

Szczerbiak, A. (2012). *Poland within the European Union: New awkward partner or new hearth of Europe?* Routledge.

Towns, A. (2002). Paradoxes of (in)equality: Something is rotten in the gender equal state of Sweden. *Cooperation and Conflict: Journal of the Nordic International Studies Association, 37*(2), 157–179.

Vukasović, D. M. (2020). Constructing a (EU)ropean identity. *The Balkans and the Western Balkans as the other*. Institute for Political Studies.

Walby, S. (2004). The European Union and gender equality: Emergent varieties of gender regime. *Social Politics: International Studies in Gender, State & Society, 11*(1), 4–29.

Warat, M. (2014). *Development of gender equality policies in Poland: A review of success and limitations* (Working Paper No. 2.2). Jagiellonian University.

Weber, B. (2019). Refugees and Islam: Representing race, rights, and cohabitation. In C. Carter, L. Steiner, & S. Allan (Eds.), *Journalism, gender and power* (pp. 205–220). Routledge.

Wojnicka, K. (2016). Masculist groups in Poland: Aids of mainstream antifeminism. *International Journal for Crime, Justice and Social Democracy, 5*(2), 36–49.

Young, B. (2000). Disciplinary neoliberalism in the European Union and gender politics. *New Political Economy, 5*(1), 77–98.

CHAPTER 6

Sexual Politics in Contemporary Europe: Resonance and Dissonance

Abstract The Conclusion provides an overview of the book's key arguments, and it provides a synopsis of our key findings. It reconsiders the role that feminism and feminist civil society actors play in law and policy framing and agenda setting at the EU. The chapter highlights the usefulness of our conceptual framework for those interested in sexual politics in various contexts.

Keywords Feminist analysis · The EU · Feminist civil society · The criminal law · The future

Our purpose in writing this book has been to start a conversation. As feminists whose work focuses on the intersections of gender, law, sexuality, mobility and power, we believe that there are some interesting developments afoot in European sexual politics that require urgent critical examination from different disciplinary perspectives. Therefore, as we conclude our analysis, we hope that our new critical feminist theoretical framework and our discussion has prompted some engagement in the academy. As we have demonstrated throughout this book, it is clear that contemporary Europe is invested in gender equality and the protection of sexual integrity. What our discussion has tried to show is that these are not easy matters to harmonise across European jurisdictions, and the

© The Author(s), under exclusive license to Springer Nature Switzerland AG 2022
S. FitzGerald and M.-L. Skilbrei, *Sexual Politics in Contemporary Europe*, https://doi.org/10.1007/978-3-030-91174-4_6

debates on the European and domestic level that we have detailed in this book, bring that into stark relief. This has become even more challenging in recent years because the EU is, at the same time, expanding it competencies and its jurisdiction.

Both prostitution and rape are contentious policy fields wherein ideas about sexuality, autonomy and the relationship between the citizen and the state are expressed and forged variously. This makes these issues different from the labour and market-related gender equality issues that the EU, until recently, has understood as gender equality. By transforming prostitution and rape into issues that can be incorporated into the EU's plans for greater European harmonisation, the EU and its institutions have moved into both the private sphere and into areas that traditionally fall under domestic legal regimes' jurisdiction.

We started this book with a reference to Jeffrey Week's (2012) book. Weeks argues that it is necessary to retain a critical approach in the face of developments that appear to be facilitate an expansion of freedom and justice. Inspired by this and Foucault's concept of governmentality, we have approached the sexual politics of the EU and its Member States mindful of the fact that developments can be both progressive and repressive and often this occurs simultaneously. We have, throughout the book, interrogated how gender and sexuality are appropriated, even weaponised, beyond the aim of securing freedom and justice for all. In short, we have demonstrated how they have served as *sitting ducks*, apt to be reworked for strategic purposes. We have also taken shifts in gender and sexuality law and policy at face value as governmental attempts to address injustice and harm in new and better ways in a situation where norms and understandings are rapidly changing. In this context, we have viewed gender and sexuality norms as *moving targets*. This is particularly important where the EU's plans for ever greater union through harmonisation, comes into direct conflict with the nation state.

Both perspectives, we have argued, are relevant and valid. Feminism has, as Walby (1999) contends, experienced great wins as the EU has applied its considerable economic and normative powers to align Member States in their investments in social justice. At the same time, it is clear that the EU throughout most of its existence has dealt with gender equality and sexual integrity only to the extent that it harms or supports productivity and labour market participation and further the EU project (see e.g. Vera-Gray & Kelly, 2020).

As we have addressed in this book, feminist civil society actors play a major role in initiating, forging, disseminating and legitimising EU's positions and policies. A question that we have returned to throughout the previous chapters is whether feminist civil society's involvement in the European project means that the feminist project has been repurposed to gloss over what is, in real terms, about access to and regulation of markets and not equality. In making the EU, and subsequently its Member States, shift positions on prostitution and rape it has been necessary to simplify and to remove the multiplicity of voices and experiences from the debate. In that process, prostitution and rape are presented as simple policy issues, without reference to differences between women in how they experience these phenomena or how the proposed policies to intervene in their regulation or criminalisation would affect them. This is most notable in the case of prostitution where the assumption that there is one feminist goal and one feminist policy permeates both the Honeyball Report, the 2014 EP Resolution and the EP's press release. Conflicts between women around what is in their interest and, thus, the possibility for policy based on an intersectional perspective, disappear. We would go as far as to say that in the race to harmonise the 'Swedish model' across the EU, feminist principles have been depoliticised of their transformative potential not for those women and men on the margins of European society but for all. On this question in her focus on sexual citizenship Josephson writes that:

> The empirical reality of public policy as it constitutes and reifies subjects is important, and why feminist engagement with public policy must also be about challenging the reified subject positions that public policy imagines and attempts to create and re-create. Reconceptualising the subject is intertwined with reconceptualising a politics that does not require a generic human, but that opens up the political and human possibilities for people of all positionalities and intersectional locations'. (2016: 27)

While Josephson's context is the United States of America, we believe that it is a critique that has analytical and political application in other contexts such as the EU while also retaining the integrity and political potential of feminist ambitions and alliances. In the past, an important battle for the women's movement was to move issues of gendered and sexualised harms from the private to the public sphere. The integrity of the female body became the nexus for second-wave feminism as it came to stand for women's autonomy and self-determination generally (Outshoorn et al., 2015: 1). In turn, this concentrated on citizenship, human rights and justice. Those issues remain salient to contemporary feminist politics and, therefore, warrant more careful scrutiny. What past feminist concerns and politics has taught us is that while these ideals were important for women at that time; their means of achieving their goals were by no means clear. Therefore, it is unsurprising that at the time feminists prioritised securing the female body and extending rights and protections to women as full citizens. The lesson from intersectional feminist analysis reveals that these goals and achievements were partial and that class and 'race' continued to play an important role in deciding 'whose voice', 'whose rights' and 'whose perspective' mattered. In most of the Western world by the late 1960s, women were recognised before the law as full citizens. They had personhood and were, at least on paper, ensured justice. But the prevailing lack of real protections and recognition of all women's autonomy spoke to a more ontological problem at the heart of feminism and social relations, and one that could explain the continued non-realisation of many women's full citizenship rights and justice.

It is in light of this that we argue that more work needs to be done in this area. Furthermore, it is because we believe that the issues we present in this book are timely and important that we ask the reader to interpret the controversies we present in this book. For us, then the critical questions become about *who* is allowed to define what equality and sexuality integrity mean and *how* to they do it.

While we have pointed to concrete examples of people, institutions and organisations that have acted at national and EU levels to shift discourses and policies on gender and sexuality, our intention is not to present shifts as the result of individual agency. But rather, we are interested in the genealogy of the discursive formation around gender and sexuality and, in particular, in how this is expressed in how prostitution and rape have come to be redefined as particular kinds of policy issues at the European level and domestic levels. In the interaction between the EU and Member States and between government bodies and civil society, we have identified the relationality between the governmental technologies and political rationalities as areas that require more critical engagement (Rose & Miller, 1992).

Core to our argument has been that we have identified how the EU and national governments attempt to govern through particular policies relative to gender and sexuality. The two policy areas we selected for this book, prostitution and rape, demonstrate the challenges that emerge when particular 'knowledge' claims around gender and sexuality permeate law and policy and assume the mantle of 'truth'. This became clear as we traced how Swedish feminist discourse and practice around prostitution entered the EU policy sphere and ultimately became hegemonic and representative of European norms and values on this question. In the process, however, feminist core principles on inclusivity and difference were obscured, silenced and rendered 'unfeminist'. As we have demonstrated in the case of the Honeyball Report, the 2014 Resolution from the EP built on the EU's intention to harmonise policies on prostitution across the Union. In doing do, it built upon discrete forms of 'knowledge' about what, in the view of certain dominant feminists, caused prostitution and which policies would work. On critical reflection, however this knowledge seems partial and strategic. Rather than support gender equality policy for all it seems to be a proxy intended to build a particular kind of feminist power base at the EU level.

In Chapter 1 we drew on historical work that identified the sexual politics of the past. Such work illustrates the value of being careful in designating something and someone as progressive and others as regressive and an enemy of feminism. Winds, however, may turn and so do minds. While contemporary discourses on sexual politics in Europe have the semblance of heavily segmented geographical differences between East–West and North–South, what we discuss in this book alludes to a new and emerging situation. Those corners of Europe that in our recent past we considered 'progressive' or 'women friendly' no longer seem so welcoming to 'difference'. A good example that illustrates this point well is how in 1964–1965, Swedish women had to go to Poland to have abortions (Freidenvall, 2015: 128–129). Abortion was illegal in Sweden at the time, available only to few upon submitting an application to the medical authorities. Freidenvall described how, at the time, 'the Swedish Prosecutor General regarded these activities as illegal and stated that it was a crime against Swedish interests to abort a Swedish foetus' (2015: 128). Travelling to Poland for abortions was not just an individual act of desperation or choice, but it was also a collectively organised political action among Swedish women. Nevertheless, it took until 1975 for

Sweden to decriminalise abortion and introduce 'free' abortion. In hindsight 'the Poland case' is believed to have spurred Swedish debates that led to the normalisation of a pro-choice position in Sweden (Freidenvall, 2015). When 20 years later Sweden joined the EU the opinion was quite different. Then one of the main arguments against joining the Union was that that might infringe upon Sweden's progressive approach to abortion and other issues to do with gender and sexuality (Freidenvall, 2015; see also Gould, 2001). By contrast, it is possible to identify countries that have expanded gender and sexuality, countries like Ireland that up to the recent past haved adopted a harsh stance in this area. What this situation demonstrates is that sexual politics in Europe is far from fixed but it is in flux.

Our aim in this book has been to offer a critical feminist analysis of the trajectory and dynamics of the EU's sexual politics. We want to prompt further dialogue on this and related issues. Therefore, we do not perceive this as the definitive answer to the questions we began by posing, but rather it is an invitation to others to join in the conversation. As we have indicated throughout the previous chapters, the EU's gender equality policies do not necessarily promoting a transformative progressive agenda, but we can see them as establishing the lowest common denominator that will at the very least keep the peace within the Union. Relevant here is Strid's (2009) point that the successes the EWL has had around influencing the EU may have come at the price of more radical agendas. Acknowledging the networked character of policy-making on prostitution and rape, we argue that EU is not the 'maker' of these policies. Instead, we submit that it is the policymaking processes that *make* the EU, and it is through these policies that it governs. This means that the kinds of expertise networks we discuss in this book play a constitutive role in imagining and determining the EU's present and its future. If the politics of gender equality and sexual integrity are 're-coupled' within their feminist origins, we can, we hope, create those necessary spaces where we can imagine and influence a more transformative law and policy around gender and sexuality that is rooted less in the criminal law and more in social justice.

Where might those conversations begin? One area that suggests immediate potential is by transforming how we think about how the laws regulating gender and sexuality as inherently good or bad. After the work of feminist legal scholar, Jane Scoular we suggest that it is useful to examine what laws *do* in a broad sense (Scoular, 2015). Another important avenue for analysis is to 'rethink', policies that appear on the surface to be progressive but may have very conservative outcomes. Liberalisation and more rights for individuals may at the outset appear to be a positive thing, but, again, looking to Hunt's (2013) point concerning how the law does not act on individuals in a straightforward way, but it is also a normalising instrument. Reminiscent of Scoular's point we reference above, is that while rape legislation has limited our power to end rape, the reason that people seek social change by prioritising law is that it infiltrates 'extra-legal sites' and, thus, forms what can and cannot be said and thought about rape (Bonnycastle, 2000: 65). This means that we need to look differently at law and at what law does, and 'not look at its sovereign expression but rather at the way legal process and norms operate, alongside other discourses, to construct the fabric of the modern subject' (Scoular, 2015: 19).

Several researchers have problematised how feminists have contributed to the strengthening of a law-and-order rather than a social justice agenda by how they, in various contexts, have argued for more prohibitions and harsher punishments for issues that are, in part, social problems (see e.g. Bonnycastle, 2000; Gruber, 2020). The example of prostitution is especially ripe for this critique. The reasons why prostitution exists and why sex workers are harmed by it, are grounded in the gendered, radicalised and classed effects of social injustice and a sexual double standard. As criminal justice is an individualising and blunt instrument the function of which is to punish, repress and condemn, it cannot, however be responsive to people's lived experiences of exploitation, or violence or indeed the social injustice and sexual double standard that creates the socio-economic and cultural conditions in which rape and prostitution flourish. In such conditions, the challenge becomes how to develop modes of conceptualisation that are open to and can be responsive to different political contexts, strengthen the momentum for progressive policy making rather than closing down those spaces and undermining the worthy principles of gender equality, sexual and human rights for all. *European Sexual Politics* offers an entry point for analysis of these questions.

REFERENCES

Bonnycastle, K. (2000). Rape uncodified: Reconsidering bill C-49 amendments to Canadian sexual assault laws. In D. E. Chunn & D. Lacombe (Eds.), *Law as a gendering practice* (pp. 60–78). Oxford University Press.

Commission of the European Communities. (1996). Communication from the Commission: Incorporating Equal Opportunities for Women and Men into All Community Policies and Activities, COM(96)67 final of 21 February 1996.

Freidenvall, L. (2015). In pursuit of bodily integrity in Sweden. In J. Outshoorn (Ed.), *European women's movements and body politics: The struggle for autonomy* (pp. 118–152). Palgrave Macmillan.

Gould, A. (2001). The criminalisation of buying sex: The politics of prostitution in Sweden. *Journal of Social Policy, 30*(3), 437–456.

Gruber, A. (2020). *The feminist war on crime: The unexpected role of women's liberation in mass incarceration.* University of California Press.

Hunt, A. (2013). Encounters with juridical assemblages: Reflections on Foucault, law and the juridical. In B. Golder (Ed.), *Rereading Foucault: On law, power and rights* (pp. 64–84). Routledge.

Josephson, J. (2016). *Rethinking sexual citizenship.* SUNY Press.

Maj, J. (2017). *Gender equality in the European Union: A comparative study of Poland and Germany.* Nomos.

Outshoorn, J., Dudová, R., Prata, A., & Freidenvall, L. (2015). Women's movement and bodily integrity. In J. Outshoorn (Ed.), *European women's movements and body politics: The struggle for autonomy* (pp. 1–21). Palgrave Macmillan.

Peters, B. G., & Pierre, J. (2009). Governance approaches. In A. Wiener & T. Diez (Eds.), *European integration theory, 2nd ed* (pp. 91–104). Oxford University Press.

Rose, N., & Miller, P. (1992). Political power beyond the state: Problematics of government. *British Journal of Sociology, 43*(2), 173–205.

Scoular, J. (2015). *The subject of prostitution: Sex work, law and social theory.* London: Routledge.

Strid, S. (2009). *Gendered interests in the European Union: The European Women's Lobby and the organisation and representation of women's interests.* Örebro University.

Vera-Gray, F., & Kelly, L. (2020). Contested gendered space: Public sexual harassment and women's safety work. In V. Ceccato & M. K. Nalla (Eds.), *Crime and fear in public places: Towards safe, inclusive and sustainable cities* (pp. 217–231). Routledge.

Walby, S. (1999). Changes in women's employment in the United Kingdom. *New Political Economy, 4*(2), 195–213.

Weeks, J. (2012). *Sex, politics and society: The regulation of sexuality since 1800.* London: Routledge.

Index

A
Abolitionists, 51
Abortion, 114, 129
Absence of consent, 80
Acquis communautaire, 79, 103
Act Prohibiting the Purchase of Sexual Services, 53
Advocacy coalition, 28
Advocacy networks, 62
Agenda-setting, 24

B
Beijing Platform for Action, 84
Biopolitics, 47
British Protocol, 111
Brussels, 76

C
Catholic Church, The, 112, 115, 116
Charter of Fundamental Human Rights, 81
Charter of Fundamental Rights, 23, 27, 111

Christian reformers, 50
Citizenship, 7, 10–12, 128
Civil society actors, 8, 24
Coalitions, 86
Commission on the Status of Women, 83
Committee on the Elimination of Discrimination against Women (CEDAW), 77, 112
Conduct of conduct, 14, 75, 81
Conduct people's conduct, 47
Consensus, 62, 63, 84
Contagious Diseases Acts (CDAs), 49
Copenhagen Criteria, 9
Council of the European Union, The, 23, 88, 106
Criminal Law Amendment Act (1885), The, 50
Cyprus, 26

D
Daphne Programme, The, 89, 90
Discrimination, 23
Domestic violence, 81

E

Eastern and Central European countries, 36
Economic rationalities, 78
Eighteenth-century, The, 46
Epistemic communities, 39, 84
Equal pay, 22
Equal work, 22
EU expansion, 39
Euro-crimes, 9, 24, 25, 75
European body politic, 82
European Commission, The, 9, 33, 88, 89
European community, 89
European Convention in Human Rights (ECHR), 34, 90
European Court of Justice (CJEU), 9
European identity, 7, 10, 20, 23, 31, 78, 82, 83, 86
European identity-formation, 82
European Institute for Gender Equality (EIGE), 108
European integration, 29
Europeanisation of public discourses, 24
Europeanness, 10
European Parliament (EP), The, 14, 23, 24, 33, 57–62, 88, 109, 129
European political identity, 3
European project, The, 5, 13
European values, 8, 10, 15, 26, 36, 65, 75, 87, 108, 113
European Women's Lobby (EWL), 33–35, 61–64, 66, 92, 94, 130

F

FEMM Committee, The, 34, 59–61, 89, 94
Femocrats, 84, 118
Femonationalism, 118
Foucault, Michel, 6, 9, 13, 25, 46, 47, 57, 78
Fourth World Conference on Women, 83
France, 48, 51, 58
Fraser, Nancy, 12
French system, The, 52

G

Gender-based violence, 81
Gender equality, 13
Gender mainstreaming, 13, 23, 79, 84, 85, 120
Genealogy, 6, 13, 47, 75, 128
German, 116
Germany, 6, 14, 63, 102, 116–119
Globalisation, 82
Governance, 3, 30
Governmentality, 29, 46–49, 51, 52, 57, 75, 78, 80, 82, 85, 93
techniques of, 48
Governmental technologies, 87, 128

H

Harmonisation, 7
Honeyball Report, The, 60, 61, 129
Human rights, 83, 128
Human trafficking, 7, 9, 25, 50, 56, 65, 66, 79, 88
Hungary, 5, 27, 120

I

Immigration control, 24, 38, 82
Immigration policy, 66
Integration theory, 29
International Abolitionist Federation (IAF), 50
International Relations, 29
Ireland, 36, 58, 63, 64, 80, 109
Islam, 10
Istanbul Convention, The, 4, 34, 90, 92, 93, 107, 110, 113–115, 118
Italy, 5, 14, 102, 105, 116

INDEX 135

J
Jurisdiction, 9, 14, 22, 26, 46, 51–53, 58, 62, 66, 78–80, 83

L
Ladies National Association (LNA), 49
Lesbian, Gay, Bisexual, Transgender, Queer and Intersex (LGBTQI), 4, 5, 27, 31, 36, 107, 111

M
#MeToo, 74
Migrants, 119
Migration, 7, 82
Modern-day sexual slavery, 7
Muslim 'other', The, 117, 118

N
National identity, 6, 20, 63, 81, 83, 103, 109, 115, 117, 119
Neo-abolitionists, 25, 57
Netherlands, The, 62, 63
New Zealand, 58
Nineteenth-century, The, 48
Nordic model, 52

O
'Others', 38
Outshoorn, Joyce, 62, 106

P
Palermo Protocol, The, 51
Paris Summit, The, 22
Parliamentary committees, 24
Pegida, 117
Poland, 4, 15, 26, 27, 87, 103, 106, 110, 112, 114, 115, 129

Policy harmonisation, 4
Policy network, 30
Polish national identity, 5
Polishness, 105
Political rationality(ies), 87, 128
Principle of equal treatment, 13
Protection, 10

R
Racialised discourse(s), 82
Radical feminist, 25
Rape, 14
 as 'coerced acts', 80
Regulation, 47
Regulationist model, The, 49
Resistance, 78
Rights, 8
Russia, 36

S
Scandinavian effect, 85
Scoular, Jane, 48
Securitisation, 24, 38, 82
Seventeenth-century, The, 11
Sexual citizenship, 10, 12, 65
Sexual exploitation, of women and children, 9
Social Action Programme, 22
Social Protocol, The, 22
Sovereignty, 5–7, 29, 102, 105
Soviet Bloc, 4
State feminism, 38
Sweden, 14, 15, 32, 37, 52, 53, 55, 57, 85, 102, 104, 106, 108, 109, 119
Swedish model, The, 54

T
1970s, 22
1980s, 22

Tolerance, 10
Treaties of Rome, 35
Treaty of Amsterdam, The, 4, 8, 23, 33, 83, 85
Treaty of Lisbon, The, 9, 21, 23, 24, 65, 66, 111
Treaty of Maastricht, The, 22, 27, 31
Treaty of Rome, The, 14, 21, 22, 75
Turn off the Red Light campaign (ToRL), 64
Twentieth-century, The, 3, 11, 52

U

UN Declaration on the Elimination of Violence against Women, 83
United Nations Human Rights High Commission (UNHRC), 83
US, The, 77

V

Velvet triangle, The, 25, 32, 33, 60, 94
Vienna Declaration and Programme of Action (VDPA), 83

W

Walby, Sylvia, 38
White slavery, 50
White slave trade, 61
Women's groups, 86
World Conference on Human Rights in Vienna, 83
World Health Organisation (WHO), 74

Printed in the United States
by Baker & Taylor Publisher Services